LET THE WEAK SAY I AM STRONG

LET THE WEAK SAY I AM STRONG

SAM McGRANER

Pathway
PRESS

Library of Congress Catalog Card Number: 98-068213

ISBN: 98-068214

◆

To my mother and father,
Martha and *Burt McGraner,*
whose "good name is to be chosen
rather than great riches,
loving favor rather than silver and gold"
(Proverbs 22:1).

◆

C✦O✦N✦T✦E✦N✦T✦S

Foreword   9

Acknowledgments   11

Introduction   13

ONE

The Nature of Weakness   19

TWO

Defining Strength   33

THREE

Strength of Conviction   43

FOUR

Strength of Character   61

FIVE

Strength of a Calling   75

SIX

Strength of Commission   89

SEVEN

Strength of Communion   101

EIGHT

Strength of Commitment   115

NINE

Strength of Compassion   131

TEN

Weakness on Purpose   145

(

FOREWORD

"Why me?" is the prevailing cry of today's troubled world. People everywhere are searching for answers to life's perplexing problems. But, more often than not, the complexities of modern life pose more questions than answers. What really are the answers to the difficulties that befall and baffle mankind? The confusing voices of religionists, politicians, psychics, gurus, and soothsayers all claim to have the answers to life's questions. However, author Sam McGraner reminds us that the only real answers are found in the timeless message of the Word of God.

Let the Weak Say I Am Strong is based on the premise that we can find the strength to face life's difficulties only by acknowledging our weakness and putting our trust in the all-encompassing strength of the Lord. It is intended to help people who find themselves overwhelmed in times of physical and spiritual weakness by showing them how several Biblical characters found strength in their own times of weakness.

The author shows the grace of God in operation in the lives of these Biblical characters as God takes what Satan meant for harm and turns it for good. Also using examples from his own ministry and his experiences growing up as the son of a preacher, McGraner illustrates how God uses times of discouragement and apparent defeat to reveal that all things do indeed work together for good.

This is an excellent book for someone who is suffering and asking, "Why?" It will help those who feel weak to find greater trust in the Lord and say, "I can do all things through Christ who strengthens me" (Philippians 4:13).

—Dennis McGuire
Assistant General Overseer

ACKNOWLEDGMENTS

Special thanks . . .

+ To my good friend and Christian brother, Homer Rhea, for supporting and encouraging me, not only in this project, but also in establishing my present ministry at Pathway Press.

+ To Wanda Griffith, book editor, whose editorial skills greatly improved and enhanced my manuscript.

+ To a loving congregation, the Wagner Avenue Church of God in Sidney, Ohio, where the ideas and insights contained in this book were birthed—and preached. You will always hold a special place in my heart.

INTRODUCTION

It has been said that the first law of nature is "Only the strong survive." However, a better rendition of that law might be, "Only the strongest survive for the moment." In a conflict between two males of a given species, the strongest prevails only to fight again and again until finally a stronger challenger arises. This victor then faces the same fate as the animal he defeated. Whether through the weakening of time or simply the superiority of his challenger, he will one day face sure defeat.

This is the sequence of nature. Strengths grow and fade, appear and vanish, leaving the weak behind. We may be more civil about it in our everyday life, but we still devise our "pecking orders." Ultimately, only the strong survive for a while.

I am not referring to physical strength, great willpower, or any other elements we associate with strength. I am referring to those who are strengthened by the Lord. Paul's exhortation to the Ephesians was, "Be strong in the Lord and in the power of His might" (Ephesians 6:10). The strength attained in the Lord is not fleeting or fickle; it is not weakened by age, hampered by illness, or subject to gender, intellect, or physical differences. It is consistent, lasting, and available to all. Ironically, the only sure way to receive this kind of strength is through the acceptance and admission of weakness. That's what this book is about.

Proverbs 18:10 says, "The name of the Lord is a strong tower; the righteous run to it and are safe." The purpose of this book is to bring encouragement during times of physical or spiritual weakness with this message: Seek the shelter of that "strong tower." It is there you will find strength.

To achieve this purpose, I have selected several Biblical characters who were vexed by weakness. Their weaknesses came from several sources—other people, time, God, or their own choices. Each study is focused, not on the condition of their weaknesses, but on the strength God revealed in them through these weaknesses. A brief synopsis of these strengths may encourage you to read further.

Strength of conviction is seen in the life of Abraham. Hearing God's voice, he left his father's house and journeyed to a land he had never seen. When God promised he would become a great nation, he believed. When God told him to take his son to a mountain and offer him as a sacrifice, he obeyed. Abraham was a man of conviction.

Strength of character is displayed in the life of Joseph.

With the injustices handed him from his brothers, Potiphar's wife, and his fellow prisoners, Joseph remained strong. His example of character is one we should all emulate.

Strength of a calling is to accept trials, conflicts, and challenges of the mind and spirit. But more than this, it is a call to accept God's strength in the work He has called us to. Moses is one of those called late in life to a seemingly impossible task. His success in fulfilling God's call will be our model for the strength of a calling.

Strength of commission is exhibited in a person who has a vision, a singular purpose. We may call these people militants or activists because they view their cause as a personal commission. Gideon was such a person. We probably would not have chosen Gideon to lead the battle against the Midianites, but God did. Why? The answer is given in Judges 7:2: "Lest Israel claim glory . . . saying, 'My own hand has saved me.'" Gideon may have been a reluctant leader, but he recognized the source of his strength of commission.

Strength of communion is the act of participating in fellowship with, or sharing in the experiences of, another. We have communion with others every day. This communion either strengthens or weakens those with whom we fellowship. But this strength of communion does not come solely from our fellowship with each other. It is primarily a by-product of communion with God. Daniel was a godly man who enjoyed communion with God three times a day without fail. He will be our example of the strength of communion.

Strength of commitment is vital in the Christian experience. It is a quality of strength God is looking for in those He has called. Paul, our example of commitment, wrote in 1 Corinthians 15:58: "Therefore, my beloved brethren, be steadfast, immovable, always abounding in the work of the Lord, knowing that your labor is not in vain in the Lord." Hebrews 3:14 states, "For we have become partakers of Christ if we hold the beginning of our confidence steadfast to the end."

Strength of compassion reveals that a person is strong enough to show mercy, strong enough to care, strong enough to forgive. The compassion of God is probably the single most vivid demonstration of His strength. Not creation, not the miracles of both Old and New Testaments—not even the coming judgment—reveal the strength of God more clearly than His compassion on sinful man. That the God who created and maintains the universe would have such compassion for us as to send His Son Jesus to die for our sins is amazing. He who could easily have destroyed it all and started over again chose to reveal a greater strength through compassion rather than the obvious strength of His might. He is looking for this same type of strength in us—for us to be loving, forgiving, and compassionate toward each other and those caught in sin. Jesus will be our supreme example of compassion.

In the following chapters I will discuss seven Biblical elements of strength revealed in each of these characters. As you will see later in the book, God sometimes allows and even inflicts a weakening of the things we consider strength in order to bring about a greater reliance upon His strength.

Just as the prophet Joel gave a "wake-up call" to the southern kingdom to "let the weak say, 'I am strong'" (3:10), this book offers the same call to God's people today to "let the weak say I am strong"—"strong in the Lord and in the power of His might" (Ephesians 6:10).

The Nature of Weakness

1

Late one summer evening, an old man found himself unable to sleep because of persistent hunger pains. Reluctantly he turned on his dim bedside lamp. Beside the lamp were three apples he had picked from the apple tree in his backyard. *An apple is exactly what I need,* he thought. He bit into the apple and discovered a worm inside. Tossing the apple out the open bedroom window, he bit into the second apple only to find that it too contained a worm. Somewhat agitated, he turned out the light, quickly ate the remaining apple, and returned to bed.

If we remain ignorant of the worms, we can enjoy the apples—that is also the nature of weakness. As long as we are unaware of them, we go along until suddenly, often tragically, we learn the truth.

Facing the Truth

We all have weaknesses. Sometimes they are concealed, or even denied, but sooner or later we must face the truth. Even one as righteous as Job admitted the truth of his weakness when he lamented, "What strength do I have?" (Job 6:11). Before calamity struck, Job probably would not have boasted about it, but surely a sense of strength rested in his heart. After all, he served God more righteously than anyone of his time. Job had a right to feel strong—God had blessed him richly with family and possessions. But deep inside, he was aware of the potential for weakness.

Part of Job's fear was evident in the fact that he regularly offered burnt offerings on behalf of his children just in case they had "cursed God in their hearts" (1:5). In rapid succession, his health, wealth, and family were taken. He declared, "For the thing I greatly feared has come upon me, and what I dreaded has happened to me" (3:25).

Weakness is defined as a period or state of being weak, brought on by any number of physical, mental, or spiritual situations. A flaw or defect in a person's character allows such situations to develop when there is an unusual fondness or desire for something.

Because weaknesses take so many forms, we can never be secure in our strengths. Paul advised, "Let him who thinks he stands take heed lest he fall" (1 Corinthians 10:12). Samson, the epitome of physical strength, had a glaring weakness for women (Judges 14—16). The mighty prophet Elijah fell prey to self-pity (1 Kings 19). The warrior David, though victorious in many battles, succumbed to lust (2 Samuel 11). The rich young ruler who came to Jesus with a burdened heart received from Jesus an invitation to follow Him, but could not accept the invitation because it was coupled with the command to "sell all that you have and distribute to the poor" (Luke 18:18-24). His riches were his strength and his weakness.

Physical Weakness

Physical weakness becomes a greater reality with age. Young people in general are oblivious to this fact. As life progresses, grim reality sets in. Not so long ago I could climb a 12-step flight of stairs in four giant steps. Now I make use of every step—and the handrail. First Peter 1:24 says, "All flesh is as grass, and all the glory of man as the flower of the grass. The grass withers, and its flower falls away."

Proper nutrition, exercise, and health care certainly delay the effects of aging, but delay is the most we can hope for. As time passes, we come to accept our aches, limps, and wrinkles.

Some weaknesses catch us by surprise. When we least expect it, illness, accidents, or other calamities leave us with weaknesses that suddenly become the focus of our attention and the agony of our lives, while the weaknesses of aging creep up on us over time. Weaknesses can take us from lives of hope and joy to lives of worry and pain in a split second.

In these situations, we tend to blame illness, misfortune, and even our own clumsiness when the true culprit is simply the weakness and frailty of life itself. From the moment our life begins as an embryo in our mother's womb, illness and death are threats. We find little consolation in the knowledge that everyone faces this same fate.

As my wife says, "Eat right, exercise, and you still die." No matter how fit we are, or how our muscles protrude, we are weak.

Spiritual Weakness

It would be useless to try to list the many spiritual weaknesses that capture people today. With innovations in our increasingly pleasure-centered world, the list is growing. We can, however, categorize these weaknesses in a very simple Biblical triad, according to 1 John 2:16:

+ The lust of the flesh
+ The lust of the eyes
+ The pride of life

Spiritual weaknesses are the product of "all that is in the world"—those things that are "not of the Father but of the world." Let's take a closer look at each of these categories.

1. *The lust of the flesh.* The lust of the flesh deals with more than just sexual immorality. Any desire that feeds the cravings of the flesh for an artificial "high" or separation from reality can be classified as the lust of the flesh. Gluttony feeds the desire for fullness and taste. And sexual immorality certainly takes its place among the many other lusts in this category.

We are human beings with fleshly desires. Consequently, we will always be subject to the weaknesses ("all that is in the world") of the flesh. We may have thighs of bronze and legs of iron, but they stand on feet of clay. Facing this truth lends a word of caution: we should not take our physical strength for granted.

The owner of a steel mill was giving a new employee

a tour of his plant. Everywhere various types of machinery were moving beams of heavy steel. In the furnace area, hot molten steel flowed from giant vats into molds. "With all the danger in this steel mill, I suppose you are very concerned when a new employee begins work," the new employee said. "No," replied the owner. "It's not the new employees that worry me; it's the old employees who have lost their fear of the steel."

We are not impervious to temptation. It is possible for the one who seems strongest to be the most susceptible. "Let him who thinks he stands take heed lest he fall" is the admonishment from 1 Corinthians 10:12.

2. *The lust of the eyes.* Someone once said, "The eyes are the windows of the soul." Vision is one of the most innocuous of the five senses. Early in our marriage my wife, Teresa, and I lived in a run-down area of a large Northeastern city. No matter which window we looked through, we saw an unappealing vista of shabby neighborhoods. The only good memory I have of this time in our lives is that we had each other. Several years later we had the privilege of living in Salida, Colorado, where our daughter, Ashley, was born. Although that was a very difficult time for me personally, I remember with great delight the joy of looking through my windows at the

beauty of the Rocky Mountains. The light coming through the windows makes a big difference on those inside.

As "windows of the soul," the light coming through our eyes will also make a big difference in our outlook, and who we are becoming. Eyes that look upon things of the world generate cravings that in most cases cannot be satisfied. Pornography creates unnatural desires and reduces God-given relationships to a base thrill that is demeaning. Even eyes that look upon creation without respect for the Creator generate a one-sided appreciation for the effect without due reverence for the Cause.

David learned the hard way how roving eyes can draw the soul astray. In Psalm 25:15 he said, "My eyes are ever toward the Lord, for He shall pluck my feet out of the net." Eyes fixed on the glories of God will not be enticed by the glitter of the world.

3. *The pride of life.* Psalm 52 speaks of the person caught up in the pride of life. In verse 1 of this contemplation David asks, "Why do you boast in evil, O mighty man?" Verse 7 says of this person, "Here is the man who did not make God his strength, but trusted in the abundance of his riches, and strengthened himself in his wickedness."

The pride of life is not so much a matter of conceit as

it is a matter of trust. Some boast in their appearance, talent, or knowledge, while others boast in their charisma or wealth. But there is an underlying factor that is common to them all. These once-strong assets become weaknesses when men and women trust them for their glory and advancement.

In this light, pride is akin to idolatry. Trusting anything more than God becomes idolatrous. We must be diligent in keeping a proper perspective lest our greatest strength becomes our greatest weakness. We are like the rich man in Luke 18 who could not come to grips with the temporal nature of the god he trusted and the eternal nature of the God he longed for.

A certain man built a great fortune. He had the finest mansion and the most expensive cars. No one—not even he—knew his worth. After a brief illness, he died. The media carried numerous reports of his death. One reporter asked the wealthy man's attorney, "How much did he really leave his family?" The attorney replied curtly, "Every last cent. He didn't take a penny with him." Edgar A. Guest wrote in his poem "What Counts":

> Most any old man can tell you,
> most any old man at all,

Who has lived through all sorts of weather,
>   winter and summer and fall,
That riches and fame are shadows that dance on
>   the garden wall.[1]

A Wrestling Match

The truth is, before the weak can say, "I am strong," the weak must admit, "I am weak." From whom should such an admission come? A better question might be, "Who among us is immune to the lust of the flesh, the lust of the eyes, and the pride of life?" This is the truth we must face.

The prophet Hosea wrote of Jacob, "In his strength he struggled with God" (Hosea 12:3). The same thing could be said of us when we struggle with God—pitting our strengths against His. Like Jacob, we come away from some of these wrestling matches with a permanent limp, learning and relearning the same lessons.

We enter these wrestling matches convinced that we know the right path and destination for our lives, but we are no match for God. During the process, we identify with David in Psalm 31:10 when he said, "My strength fails because of my iniquity, and my bones waste away." In 38:10 he lamented, "My heart pants, my strength fails me; as for the light of my eyes, it also has gone from me."

Whatever strengths we had were lost in the struggle. Thinking we were on the right road with direction from God, we find ourselves in direct opposition to God's plan and will. In the end we are chastised for our error.

God is never harsh or vindictive when He saps our strength—He is simply being Father. And a good father knows what strength really is. An illustration of this is seen in two bumper stickers. One father, aware of the strength of knowledge, places a bumper sticker on his car that reads, "MY KID IS AN HONOR STU-DENT." Another father, who is not so wise about what strength is, places a bumper sticker on his car that reads, "MY KID CAN BEAT UP YOUR HONOR STUDENT."

God intends for every struggle or wrestling match to work for our good (see Romans 8:28) because He knows what strength really is. He also knows our make-up. David wrote in Psalm 103:13, 14, "As a father pities his children, so the Lord pities those who fear Him. For He knows our frame; He remembers that we are dust." Understanding our nature and our need, God wrestles with us for a purpose. He has a wonderful plan for our lives. It may take some polishing and refining, but He sees in you and me a divine purpose we cannot see.

Earthen Vessels

The high school I attended in the mountains of Kentucky was poorly funded and equipped even for the 1960s. It was quite an achievement when our art teacher acquired a small kiln to start a class in ceramics. As a member of that first class, I learned valuable lessons that have been crucial to potters over the centuries. There are many opportunities for failure in the production of an earthen vessel. Impurities in the clay will cause it to break apart in the heat of the kiln. So the potter cuts and compacts the clay many times until all the impurities are gone. If the clay were able to think, it would probably wonder why the potter is so angry. But the potter goes through this process for the good of the clay, that the vessel be made of purer stuff.

Isn't that what we go through as well? God wants us to be made of "purer stuff," so He allows us to go through grueling processes to drive out impurities. So we are not ignorant of our imperfections, God allows us to see the "worms in the apples." In order for us to see our need for transformation, He lets us see ourselves as clay.

When the vessel is formed, it dries to a consistency of hardened mud. It is then placed into the kiln and baked at a high temperature for several hours. The result is a red-looking vessel that is still unfit for its intended use. The heat has hardened it; it has been transformed in nature, but it is still clay.

The potter then paints the vessel with a glaze that looks more like water mixed with dust than the final color it will be. And back into the heat of the kiln it goes. The thoughts of the clay (if it could think) once again might be, "Why? What have I done to deserve this harsh treatment?" Again the heat of the kiln does its transforming work. In several hours, there emerges from the kiln a beautiful, colorful, glossy vessel.

The clay has gone through quite a transformation from mud to a beautiful vessel, but essentially all the old qualities are still there. The earthen vessel is never far from the earth from which it came. The same can be said for each of us. God has done great things in our lives, yet we are only one step away from the clay from which we were formed. We are indeed earthen vessels.

Made for Treasure

If we are to remain so close to the earth like the earthen vessel, why does God put us through such a grueling process? The answer is because the vessel itself is not the end result of the potter's work . . . it is the treasure that the vessel is made to receive.

> For we do not preach ourselves, but Christ
> Jesus the Lord, and ourselves your bondser-
> vants for Jesus' sake. For it is the God who
> commanded light to shine out of darkness,
> who has shone in our hearts to give the light
> of the knowledge of the glory of God in the
> face of Jesus Christ. But we have this treas-
> ure in earthen vessels, that the excellence
> of the power may be of God and not of us (2
> Corinthians 4:5-7).

In spite of our weaknesses, God has ordained us to be
filled with the treasure of the knowledge of Jesus Christ. An
awareness that we are earthen vessels and are subject to the
weaknesses of the flesh can only enhance our appreciation
of the power of God as He imparts to us the treasures of
His grace. In this thought, Paul found reason to glory:

> Therefore most gladly I will rather boast in my
> infirmities, that the power of Christ may rest upon
> me. Therefore I take pleasure in infirmities, in
> reproaches, in needs, in persecutions, in distresses,
> for Christ's sake. For when I am weak, then I am
> strong (2 Corinthians 12:9, 10).

We look at our strengths as gifts from God, when it
would be more accurate to look at our weaknesses as
gifts God gives us so that He might receive glory in us.

A little girl and her parents decided to visit the zoo. As

she always did, the little girl had her dad carry her on his shoulders so she could see over the crowds and the fences. Her father tired of this extra weight after a while and wanted to put the little girl down to walk. "Little girls need to learn to walk on their own," he told her. "But Daddy," she responded, "God made little girls little so they will have to sit on their daddy's shoulders to see." Never grieve about weaknesses. They are there to make us want to "sit on Daddy's shoulders."

T ✦ W ✦ O

Defining Strength

W omen are sometimes referred to as the "weaker sex," implying that men have superior strength. But typically mothers take primary responsibility in rearing children, especially when both parents work outside the home. In most Christian homes we see the mother also taking the spiritual leadership role. She manages the home, family, and her job while tending to her husband's needs. It seems that men pride themselves as being the stronger sex based upon physical strength alone, something in which any ape is by far our superior. Something is wrong with our definition of strength.

In situations requiring brute force, the person with enough physical power to do the task seems strong.

Where endurance is required, we look for someone with tenacity to exemplify strength. The person with training and experience in specific areas will appear strong in areas where knowledge is needed. However we define it, strength is relative to the circumstance. Strength in one circumstance may be more akin to weakness in another. We may be forceful enough to drive a round peg through a square hole, but is that strength? We may be cunning enough to convince someone else into doing what we want done, but is that strength? What we consider strength in one set of circumstances has the capacity to become a weakness under different circumstances.

Admirable Qualities

History is replete with accounts of heroic achievements by ordinary men and women whose personal strengths surfaced during struggles. With a measure of personal integrity and a sincere cause, most people can rise to a new level of excellence and strength.

One such quality is *self-control*, or *willpower*—that grit-your-teeth-and-bear-it, keep-a-stiff-upper-lip kind of strength. Sir Winston Churchill once said, "The bulldog's nose is pushed back so that he can breathe while he holds on with his teeth." Some compared Churchill's appearance to that of a bulldog, but he saw another worthy comparison.

When we look at Mr. Churchill, we see a short, heavy-set, bald man with a pug nose and a taste for cigars. Place him behind a butcher's counter at a supermarket and he looks right at home. Place him in a sports arena and he assumes the appearance of a typical fan. He would not even look out of place behind a hot dog vending machine on a street corner. But put him at the helm of a nation engulfed in war with Germany, and you have a "bulldog" who bites down and holds on, giving an entire nation—if not the world—a dose of his willpower for survival. Churchill possessed an admirable quality of strength, and England was blessed of God to have him at the right place at the right time.

Self-control is a quality similar to willpower that keeps one cool in a heated moment. Those who maintain self-control in difficult circumstances stand out like the Rock of Gibraltar in the midst of a storm.

Another admirable quality is *leadership*. This quality, however, cannot be reduced to a single element in every circumstance. Some become leaders because of their shrewd tactics and manipulative power over others. Some become leaders because they are articulate, persuasive, and can influence people to follow them. Still others become leaders because they are driven by a zeal for a particular cause.

Whatever the reasons, leadership is a strength that pulls together various segments of society and unites their efforts. God uses the leadership qualities of men to bring about His will. Paul said, "Let every soul be subject to the governing authorities. For there is no authority except from God, and the authorities that exist are appointed by God" (Romans 13:1).

In our fast-paced society, *patience* is a quality that is greatly admired. Traffic moves too slowly. In fact, we can define the term "split second" as the interval between the light turning green and the sound of the first horn honking. Could this be the intention of Daniel's prophecy when he said, "Many shall *run* to and fro"? (12:4).

Patience brings an aura of strength . . . someone strong enough to wait. With it a person seems to have a grip on the world, rather than being gripped by it. This makes most of us want to scream, "How can you be so calm? Are you on medication?"

God has blessed us with these and numerous other qualities we can easily classify as strengths—honesty, morality, ingenuity. We should never look at human strengths as being the ideal because they are subject to many variables, as well as our own flawed nature. These are certainly admirable qualities, but a more important concept of strength to consider is God's concept of strength.

God's Concept of Strength

God's strength is beyond our comprehension. He said, "For My thoughts are not your thoughts, nor are your ways My ways. . . . For as the heavens are higher than the earth, so are My ways higher than your ways, and My thoughts than your thoughts" (Isaiah 55:8, 9). By discovering what mankind holds in high regard, we can know what he considers to be strength. It is reasonable to believe, then, that by discovering those things on which God places a high value, we can know what He considers to be strengths in His creation.

The seven elements of strength listed in the Introduction make up the core of God's strength revealed in believers. We understand God to be omnipotent (all-powerful), omniscient (all-knowing), and omnipresent (present everywhere). These attributes of God are beyond the capacity of mankind. Only God can be God. But as God demonstrates His nature beyond these supreme attributes, elements emerge that are within the realm of human possibility. A genuine relationship with God invariably produces these elements in the life of a believer.

God is holy. Impurity finds no place within the nature of God. Therefore, when we have a nurturing relationship with God, our character is strengthened by His holiness. Christian character is more than moral standards, ethics, and mere conscience. It is a reflection of godliness in the life of the godly—a measure of the heavenly revealed in the earthly.

God is faithful. There is no wavering in the heart and mind of God. His knowledge of all things past, present, and future, combined with His supreme wisdom, gives Him unquestionable certainty of the directions we must take in every situation. He is faithful to communicate those directions to us through the means of convictions. Conviction calls us to salvation and thus to a new direction (or redirection) for our lives. Through the tool of conviction, God communicates His will for our future to us.

God is active. Colossians 1:17 says, "In him all things hold together" (*NIV*). The impact of this statement is phenomenal when you consider that without God's continued interest in the universe, it would cease to exist. As keen as His interest is in the universe, God is even more interested in the fulfillment of His will in the lives of His children. Therefore, God challenges men and women to become the channels through which He fulfills His will on earth.

God calls all men and women to serve Him, but He calls particular men and women to become servants for Him. This was the case for me, as I will relate in chapter 5.

Also, God often commissions us to perform particular tasks—to be in the right place at the right time.

God is unfaltering. He has made a complete and uncompromising commitment to those who serve Him. To illustrate the measure of commitment God holds for us, Paul stated:

> What then shall we say to these things? If God is for us, who can be against us? He who did not spare His own Son, but delivered Him up for us all, how shall He not with Him also freely give us all things? Who shall bring a charge against God's elect? It is God who justifies. Who is he who condemns? It is Christ who died, and furthermore is also risen, who is even at the right hand of God, who also makes intercession for us. Who shall separate us from the love of Christ? Shall tribulation, or distress, or persecution, or famine, or nakedness, or peril, or sword? As it is written: "For Your sake we are killed all day long; we are accounted as sheep for the slaughter." Yet in all these things we are more than conquerors through Him who loved us. For I am persuaded that neither death nor life, nor angels nor principalities nor powers, nor things present nor things to come, nor height nor depth, nor any other created thing, shall be able to separate us from the love of God which is in Christ Jesus our Lord (Romans 8:31-39).

God desires to engender this type of commitment in every believer.

God is interactive. He created us for this purpose. In the garden He enjoyed communing with Adam. He still desires to commune with His people. This is how He imparts understanding, vision, and spiritual strength to us. In this sense, communion with God is a strength in and of itself. This interaction, however, does not benefit God as much as it does the one communing with Him.

God cares. I enjoy almost all styles of Christian music, but few modern songs express the compassion of God as well as the old hymn by Frank E. Graeff "Does Jesus Care?" When the question arises within my heart, "Does God really care about me and my needs?" the answer rings in my memory as I listen to George Beverly Shea sing:

> O yes, He cares, I know He cares,
> His heart is touched with my grief;
> When the days are weary,
> The long nights dreary,
> I know my Savior cares.

The Bible declares that "love is of God," and that "God is love" (1 John 4:7, 8). Not only does God care, but He is the artisan who sculpted the pattern from which all pure forms of love and compassion are derived. We love and care because we are made in His image to reflect His love and compassion. In view of the adulteration and contamination of this divine attribute by the world, God considers pure and undefiled compassion among men and women a very real strength.

Who Is Strong?

Who is strong? My wife often quotes Erma Bombeck, who said: "People are like teabags; they don't know their own strength until they get into hot water." This is especially true for Christians. In fact, God often heats the water to bring out His strength in us. He allows circumstances to develop around us, which entice these elements of strength to surface and grow. Ironically, in the midst of a struggle with our own weakness, God's strength emerges, revealing the dramatic contrast between the two. From such a juxtaposition of our weakness and His strength, faith and hope are born.

In the following chapters I will explore the lives and circumstances of the Biblical figures mentioned in the Introduction. They were either weak at the start or were considerably weakened in the process that God led them through to produce the strength their story illustrates. In each case God proclaimed strength out of weakness.

Strength of Conviction

O n my 40th birthday I received several gifts lauding the fact that I was "over the hill." Recently I saw a response to that allegation written on a sweatshirt that read, "Over what hill? I don't remember any hill."

Whether you remember it or not, there is a point in life when you begin a downward slope toward life's end. Just when this time catches you is probably a matter of genetics, lifestyle, and attitude, but it will take place before the age of 75. At 75 you will probably be looking for ways to wind down your obligations and take life a little easier. You will enjoy playing with your grandchildren and great-grandchildren and will have no interest (or capability) in starting a new family of your own. That is, unless your name is Abram and God has just spoken to you.

We are not given complete access to the conversation between God and Abram. But the conversation was of such life-changing value that at age 75, Abram developed a dynamic conviction in his life. We are simply told in Genesis 12:1-4:

> Now the Lord had said to Abram: "Get out of your country, from your family and from your father's house, to a land that I will show you. I will make you a great nation; I will bless you and make your name great; and you shall be a blessing. I will bless those who bless you, and I will curse him who curses you; and in you all the families of the earth shall be blessed." So Abram departed as the Lord had spoken to him, and Lot went with him. And Abram was seventy-five years old when he departed from Haran.

Why would God wait until Abram was this age before calling him to a drastic change in his life? There is no way of knowing the answer, but I believe it must have something to do with Abram's strength of conviction. I see Abram as a man who, once convinced of something, held relentlessly to his conviction. This quality seems to improve with age. Someone who is labeled a "stubborn old coot" holds a stronger conviction than his or her younger component. At age 75, Abram's convictions developed into action. In the weakness of old age, God called Abram to a new strength.

The Building of a Conviction

How is conviction developed? Is it a revelation, or a process? It probably happens both ways, depending on the person involved. For Abram, it took time.

Abram was obviously a leader. Even his nephew Lot didn't question when Abram announced that God had called him to a distant land. Lot simply folded his tents and fell in line with Abram's caravan. Throughout recorded Scripture, Abram is held in high esteem. Although he made mistakes, he was not ridiculed or mocked. There is an aura about him that indicates stability. For this kind of person, convictions are developed at a pace more deliberate than others. Stephen must have understood Abram's pace when he spoke of him in Acts 7:2-4:

> Brethren and fathers, listen: The God of glory appeared to our father Abraham when he was in Mesopotamia, before he dwelt in Haran, and said to him, "Get out of your country and from your relatives, and come to a land that I will show you."

> Then he came out of the land of the Chaldeans
> and dwelt in Haran. And from there, when his
> father was dead, He moved him to this land in
> which you now dwell.

Note the progression in Stephen's message. God spoke to Abram in Mesopotamia, which prompted him to move to Haran. God continued to speak to him there. After Abram's father died, he made a dynamic move of faith, setting out in complete obedience to God.

Place yourself in Abram's shoes for a moment. You are living in a land where the people including your father (according to Joshua 24:2) worship the moon-god. At the center of your city, Ur, is a gigantic temple and a ziggurat tower erected in honor of this supposed deity. How is God going to transform you to make you willing to abandon this familiar environment for the unknown?

James 2:23 says (quoting Genesis 15:6), "'Abraham believed God, and it was accounted to him for righteousness.' And he was called the friend of God." In 2 Chronicles 20:7 we read that Abraham was called "[God's] friend forever." God sought him out . . . He initiated the relationship and revealed Himself as Abraham's friend.

This is grace at work. The God of grace sought out Abram, a man ignorant of God, to share with him His love and fellowship. Likewise, God sought me out and befriended me. He chose me long before I knew Him. The same grace that drew Abraham draws you and me into relationship today.

In the process of communication and time, Abram developed a trust in the voice of God. He developed a conviction that would move him, at the urging of God's voice, in the direction of Canaan. His convictions prompted him to believe the promises he received while journeying toward a place he did not know, but would recognize as the right place.

Abram's Convictions

It is not enough to simply say we believe—we must act upon those beliefs accordingly. To know what we believe is to place in an orderly fashion the tenets of our beliefs and consider them carefully in order to make a confession of faith. This orderly statement of faith is commonly known as a creed. Did Abram have a creed? He probably did not have a written statement of faith, but written upon his heart were the promises of God. His life was guided by his conviction from the day he left Haran to the realization of every promise.

The heritage promise. God promised Abram that He would make him a great nation. To do this, Abram must

become a father. This was at the core of God's promises
to Abram because he and Sarai had been unable to
become parents. Sometimes, God withholds the ultimate
blessing until the proper time within His plan for our
life. This was the case with Abram. It was not yet time
for him to have a son. The first step in building Abram's
great nation was to build a great name.

What is a "great name"? What is the difference
between fame, infamy, and greatness? Most importantly,
isn't it the man who makes the name great? The latter
question is at the center of Abram's strength of conviction because God promised to make the name of Abram
great. In this, two observations are in order:

1. The concept of greatness in this circumstance
would be God's, not man's. Abram's greatness would
not be founded upon great fortune or the frivolity of
public opinion—it was based on God's favor.

2. God alone would produce this greatness in
Abram's life. Abram's responsibility was to believe.

Does this sound familiar? Paul echoes this in his writings:

> For by grace you have been saved through faith,
> and that not of yourselves; it is the gift of God
> (Ephesians 2:8).

> Therefore it is of faith that it might be according

to grace, so that the promise might be sure to all the seed, not only to those who are of the law, but also to those who are of the faith of Abraham, who is the father of us all (as it is written, "I have made you a father of many nations") in the presence of Him whom he believed—God, who gives life to the dead and calls those things which do not exist as though they did; who, contrary to hope, in hope believed, so that he became the father of many nations, according to what was spoken, "So shall your descendants be" (Romans 4:16-18).

Again we see an example of God's grace in operation in Abram's life. God counted his faith, his conviction, as righteousness because he believed.

God exalted the name of Abram in spite of a serious flaw in his strategy. On two occasions when Abram traveled to Egypt and to Gerar (Genesis 12; 20), he asked Sarai to say that she was his sister because he feared the men of those nations might kill him and take her. This might be called a "half truth" because Sarai was indeed his half sister. The degree of Abram's error in these situations is open to debate, but God used each situation to enlarge the name of Abram. Both Pharaoh and Abimelech, the rulers of these countries, took Sarai into their harems. But God brought afflictions on both households and revealed the true relationship of Abram and Sarai. After Sarai was returned to him, Abram's name was reverenced by both nations.

In bestowing greatness to Abram, God changed his name from *Abram,* "exalted father," to *Abraham,* "father of many" (Genesis 17:5). In making this change, the emphasis was not placed on Abraham, but on his offspring. As time and events unfold, the name "Abraham" was exalted not only because of God's blessing upon the man but also because of the testimony of countless generations to come. Sarai's name was also changed to Sarah (17:15).

When Abraham was almost 100 years old and Sarah was 90, God reaffirmed the promise made to him 25 years before in Haran. Abraham laughed at the idea of a man and woman their age bearing a child (see Genesis 17:17). As the time of promise arrived, God appeared again to Abraham with the news that Sarah would bear a son "according to the time of life," that is, in approximately nine months. Overhearing this promise, this time Sarah laughed at such an unlikely event (18:1-15).

At the time God had specified, Sarah gave birth to Isaac, which means "he laughs." Abraham's conviction that God would give him and Sarah a child was realized. With the fulfillment of that promise came laughter. The "great nation" had begun; Abraham would leave his great name as a heritage.

The blessing promise. Obedience to God's direction has always carried with it a promise of blessing. The blessings may come in unexpected ways. Abraham waited 25 years for the birth of Isaac and the beginning of the heritage promise. The completion of God's promises of blessing would extend through centuries and millennia.

"I will bless you" were the words God spoke to Abraham. What did this mean to Abraham? To answer this question, we look at God's blessings prior to the time of Abraham. The first pronouncement of blessing was not upon man, but upon fish and fowl on the day of their creation: "And God blessed them, saying, 'Be fruitful and multiply, and fill the waters in the seas, and let birds multiply on the earth'" (Genesis 1:22). Following this, God blessed Adam and Eve:

> Then God blessed them, and God said to them, "Be fruitful and multiply; fill the earth and subdue it; have dominion over the fish of the sea, over the birds of the air, and over every living thing that moves on the earth (1:28).

Then came the blessing of the seventh day of the week: "Then God blessed the seventh day and sanctified it, because in it He rested from all His work which God had created and made" (2:3). Later a blessing was given to Noah and his family: "So God blessed Noah and his sons, and said to them: 'Be fruitful and multiply, and fill the earth'" (9:1).

In each instance the blessing included abundance, dominion, and fruitfulness. With the exception of the Sabbath blessing, the intent of God's blessing was to prosper, produce, and possess. Abraham understood God's blessing of prosperity and followed it with a strong conviction.

The blessing upon Abraham was obviously more than a promise of material prosperity. As H. Ross Perot once said, "Don't base your happiness upon things—things break." The context of God's blessing upon Abraham might be understood better by looking at the blessing God instructed the priests to pronounce upon the people of Israel in their worship:

> "Speak to Aaron and his sons, saying, 'This is the way you shall bless the children of Israel. Say to them: "The Lord bless you and keep you; the Lord make His face shine upon you, and be gracious to you; the Lord lift up His countenance upon you, and give you peace"'" (Numbers 6:22-26).

Obviously, God's blessing included more than material blessing for Abraham. With this blessing came divine protection, peace, favor, grace, and glory. Abraham was never disappointed in God's fulfillment of His promise.

God's blessing to Abraham was four-dimensional, only one of which was specifically addressed to Abraham. Three were meant for those outside the "great nation" God would make of Abraham's descendants. Notice again the exact words God spoke in Genesis 12:2, 3:

> "I will bless you . . . and you shall be a blessing. I will bless those who bless you, and I will curse him who curses you; and in you all the families [peoples, *NIV*] of the earth shall be blessed."

God's call to Abraham was for the expressed purpose of blessing others. The God of the Old Testament is the same as the God of the New Testament, and John 3:16 is closely related to Genesis 12:2, 3. Abraham was called to a different world so that the inhabitants would be blessed through him. Those who accepted and blessed him would be blessed; those who rejected and cursed him would be cursed.

There were three aspects to the blessing that would come through Abraham. The first aspect was "You shall be a blessing." Though we are not told all the qualities that made Abraham a blessing to his immediate neighbors, one example stands out in Scripture when Abraham and 318 of his trained servants defeated four kings, delivered them captives, and recovered the plunder (see Genesis 14).

The more dynamic and measurable blessings, however, would not come to the nations through Abraham the warrior, but through Abraham the servant of God. How odd it must have looked to the inhabitants of the land to see a man build an altar and burn sacrifices to an invisible God. Abraham must have been the subject of jokes until they saw how he prospered. The wells he dug continually struck water; his flocks dined on rich pasture and birthed healthy young; and anyone who entered into covenant with him shared the same fortune. An appreciation must have developed for this traveler and for the invisible God he worshiped.

In this sense, Abraham was the first missionary. Missionaries must have at least two deeply held convictions: (1) that God calls them to particular mission fields and (2) that their presence in those fields have positive effects. We know that Abraham was sure of God's calling to Canaan, but what about his conviction that he would have a positive effect there? Was Abraham following God solely because of God's promise to bless him? I don't think so.

From the beginning, Abraham held open, corporate worship in the nations where he dwelled. He built altars, offered sacrifices, and proclaimed the God whom he worshiped. After winning the battle of the kings mentioned earlier, Abraham was faced with an opportunity to confiscate the wealth gained in the battle. His response was:

> "I have raised my hand to the Lord, God Most High, the Possessor of heaven and earth, that I will take nothing, from a thread to a sandal strap, and that I will not take anything that is yours, lest you should say, 'I have made Abram rich'" (Genesis 14:22, 23).

His high principles and morality were attributed to his relationship with God.

Abraham went to Canaan with the same approach that modern missionaries go to nations of the world. They cannot become assimilated into the culture of the nation, nor should they expect the people to abandon their culture. The missionary goes to "be a blessing" and allow that blessing to become a witness for God. In this respect, the humanitarian mission cannot be separated from the religious mission; therefore, being a blessing must surely come before being a messenger.

Based upon God's promises, Abraham's convictions led him to believe that his presence would bring the promised blessings to Canaan. Abraham would be a blessing. Many would drink from the wells he dug, enjoy the refreshing rains that would follow him, and eat the fruitful harvests that came as a result of his presence. Only once would this be different because of his lack of faith (see Genesis 12:10-20). When faced with a famine, rather than wait upon God's provision, he traveled to Egypt. This was when he became involved in the controversy surrounding his relationship to Sarah. It is interesting to note that after this misdirected excursion into Egypt, Abraham traveled back to Bethel, the place where he first camped in Canaan. He was returning to his mission field, his place of blessing.

The second aspect of the blessing Abraham was to bring was "I will bless those who bless you, and I will curse him who curses you." This is also mirrored in New Testament Scripture. When Jesus sent His disciples out to preach the good news of the Kingdom, He gave them these instructions:

> Now whatever city or town you enter, inquire who in it is worthy, and stay there till you go out. And when you go into a household, greet it. If the household is worthy, let your peace come upon it. But if it is not worthy, let your peace return to you. And whoever will not receive you nor hear your words, when you depart from that house or city,

shake off the dust from your feet. Assuredly, I say to you, it will be more tolerable for the land of Sodom and Gomorrah in the day of judgment than for that city! (Matthew 10:11-15).

God's promise to Abraham was similar: "I will bless those who bless you, and I will curse him who curses you." Again, Abraham's call to the nations is given a missionary tone. Modern missionaries today must depend upon God's blessing and defense, as Abraham did.

The third and most important aspect of the blessing Abraham would bring to the nations is far-reaching. In fact, this blessing allows us to have a relationship with God. God told Abraham "in you all the families ["peoples," *NIV*] of the earth shall be blessed." This is viewed as a messianic prophecy in that the blessing will come *in* Abraham and not *by* him personally. In this simple statement, God began to reveal His plan of salvation. It would be through Abraham that God's plan would unfold.

Again we may ask, "Did Abraham understand God's intentions to bless the world through him?" "All the families [or peoples] of the earth" is quite understandable. This includes everyone . . . no exceptions. Abraham obviously held the conviction that God would bless the entire world through him. This really does eliminate the narrow view that Abraham's faith and vision were solely for his descendants, when the last word of the blessing includes all nations.

Measuring Your Strength

Abraham's heart was moved by a conviction, which moved his feet as well. Conviction that reaches to your heart and rebounds to your feet and hands produces strength that God values.

A little introspection is needed here. We must honestly search our conscience and evaluate our convictions. What do we believe God is expecting? How well do we measure up to these expectations? Remember that there is only a short step from accepting a conviction to fulfilling it.

My heart O Lord, though clear to You,
Is often dim in my earthy view.
With work and chores and cares beside,
I have little time to look inside.
Cause me somehow to stop a while,
To take account and reconcile,
That I may see Your inscriptions there,
Your commands, Your will, Your call to prayer.
And as conviction stirs and shadows flee,
Help me become what I've known I should be.
—Sam McGraner

4

Strength of Character

"You must have dark to show light; without darkness, light cannot shine." These are the words of an artist on a television program I saw several years ago. With these words, he began to paint a lighted candle in a brass candlestick on a black canvas. When he finished, the canvas was aglow with the warm light of a candle in a dark room. "To achieve this effect," he pointed out, "you must first paint the entire canvas black. Only out of darkness can you create such brilliant light."

There are times in our lives when God, in order to bring out the special glow of His strength, allows darkness to cover our lives like black paint on a canvas. During these dark times, we have no idea what God intends to bring out of this metaphoric "canvas" we call life. In fact, it becomes difficult to hope for a more colorful future when every brush stroke is filled with black paint. This abiding promise from God's Word gives us hope and encouragement to keep going: "All things work together for good to those who love God, to those who are the called according to His purpose" (Romans 8:28).

Trials come to test our faith, determination, and stamina; but like gold in the refiner's fire, character emerges through every trial.

Bright Beginnings

Joseph had a promising future. He was the favorite son of his father, Jacob, being the "son of his old age" (Genesis 37:3) and the first child borne to Jacob's greatest love, Rachel. Jacob's love for Joseph was demonstrated by the "tunic of many colors" he made for him. This close-knit relationship between father and son engendered a bond of trust and confederation that gave Joseph a sense of responsibility beyond his youth. When the sons of Bilhah and the sons of Zilpah did not perform their duties in the best interest of their father, Joseph felt compelled to bring a "bad report" of their activities to Jacob (v. 2). Later we see where Jacob sent Joseph to check on his brothers as they tended the flocks (v. 14).

Joseph's dreams also provided him with hope for a

bright future. He dreamed that while gathering and binding sheaves of grain, his brothers' sheaves bowed down to his. In another dream, the sun, moon, and 11 stars bowed down to him. The obvious implications of his dreams were that someday his brothers, his father and mother would bow to him in reverence. Such dreams brought rebuke from his father and repercussions from his brothers.

During this stage of his life, Joseph's primary strength came from his family, his father's wealth, and the close relationship he shared with him. This formed a warm security blanket that insulated him from the world. In spite of the callous treatment and harsh words of his jealous brothers, he felt protected.

It seems fitting that this family dwelled in tents. A loosened rope here, a dislodged stake there, and the tent collapses. As much as we would like to think of our family as a rock-solid fortress, it is more akin to a tent. A rebellious child, a marital conflict, sibling clashes, or any other calamity shakes a home like a tent in high wind. In spite of its strengths, the family unit is still fragile. Joseph was about to learn this painful truth.

A Subtle Darkness

Growing up in the mountains of Kentucky, one of my favorite pastimes was exploring the hills and caves surrounding my home. I really enjoyed hiking in areas I had not visited before. There were a few times when I became so involved in my exploring that before I knew it, daylight was fading and darkness was about to catch me. Not being quite as brave after dark as I was in daylight, I would make a dash toward home.

Darkness is like that. It creeps upon us and catches us unaware of its darkening shadows. Joseph was unprepared when the darkest day of his life sprang upon him like a wild animal. Warning signs were numerous, but Joseph could not imagine such betrayal from his brothers.

The beginning of Joseph's dark days came as a result of the doting affection of Jacob. His preference of Joseph spawned hatred in Joseph's brothers. Over time, this hatred grew as we see in the Biblical account in Genesis 37:4: "But when his brothers saw that their father loved him more than all his brothers, they hated him and could not speak peaceably to him." After Joseph revealed his dream of his brothers' sheaves of grain bowing to his, "they hated him even more" (vv. 5, 8).

Following Joseph's report of the second dream in which the sun, moon, and 11 stars bowed to him, "his brothers envied him" (v. 11). This animosity might have been passed off as sibling rivalry, but these were grown men with a growing hatred and jealousy of their younger brother.

At Jacob's request, Joseph traveled to where his brothers were in Dothan to check on their well-being and the condition of the flocks. The hatred reached a boiling point and the brothers contrived a plan.

> Now when they saw him afar off, even before he came near them, they conspired against him to kill him. Then they said to one another, "Look, this dreamer is coming! Come therefore, let us now kill him and cast him into some pit; and we shall say, 'Some wild beast has devoured him.' We shall see what will become of his dreams!" (Genesis 37:18-20).

They would have followed through with their plan to kill Joseph, but Ruben, who hoped to free Joseph later, convinced them to hold him in an empty cistern. But while Ruben was attending to other business, a caravan of Ishmaelites came by on their way to Egypt. For 20 pieces of silver they sold Joseph to the Ishmaelites as a slave. In one day, with one heartless act, the things Joseph considered strength were taken—his home, family, heritage, even his tunic of many colors. Everything was gone, leaving him with the bonds of a slave.

During riots or raids, the raging mob not only steals the possessions, but they also destroy everything of any emotional or sentimental value left behind. That is the kind of thief Satan is. His goal is to deprive us of our strength and see the "image" of God suffer. Though the darkness crept upon him, there was nothing subtle about Joseph's suffering.

Darker Still

Joseph probably reacted the same way I would in the same situation: wanting to escape, mourning his losses, and then calculating his assets. Joseph found that he still had his good name, his character, and his faith. He was Joseph, the son of Jacob, the son of Isaac, and the son of Abraham. Though he was still a boy (17 years old), he held to his high moral character and belief in the God of his fathers. Everything else belonged to someone else, including his life.

Upon reaching Egypt, the Ishmaelites sold Joseph to Potiphar, one of Pharaoh's officers who served as captain of the guard. Joseph chose to focus on his strengths—his good name, his character, and his faith—to build hope for the future. During the time spent in Potiphar's house, Joseph's character remained strong. He became so successful in Potiphar's house that "his master saw that the Lord was with him and that the Lord made all he did to prosper in his hand. So Joseph found favor in his sight, and served him. Then he made him overseer of his house, and all that he had he put under his authority" (Genesis 39:2-4). The name *Joseph*, though it was the name of a slave, would now be spoken with honor.

Just as the hatred and jealousy of his brothers threatened Joseph's life, he now faced the obsession of Potiphar's wife. In her lust she "cast longing eyes on Joseph, and she said, 'Lie with me'" (v. 7). This was not a single enticement. She pursued Joseph "day by day" (v. 10). Again the character of Joseph stood out as he refused her advances. Finally, alone in the house with Joseph, she attempted to force him to fulfill her wish. Grasping his garment, she pulled him toward her. Rather than giving in to her, Joseph ran, leaving his garment behind.

Various images stand out as monuments to human strength and endeavor. Neil Armstrong's footprint etched in the dust of the moon reminds us that "we can do it if we try." The mental image of Potiphar's wife clutching Joseph's garment speaks highly of Joseph's personal integrity. His rejection had little to do with her because Joseph determined to remain strong.

Injustice and success can have equally adverse effects on a person. Injustice can produce bitterness, and success can produce callousness. Both threaten our standards. This was not so with Joseph. Setting aside the hurt suffered at his brothers' hands, Joseph rose to top management within

Potiphar's house and retained his noble character. He clung to his good name, his character, and his faith more tightly than Potiphar's wife clung to his garment.

If Satan could not steal Joseph's integrity, he would have to be content with stealing his good name. Potiphar's wife, now armed with the incriminating evidence of Joseph's garment, avenged her pride by accusing Joseph of attempted rape. There was little Joseph could do. His good name was gone, and with it went his freedom. His only assets now were his character and his faith.

Darkest Before Dawn

No one is immune to hard times. Alone and demoralized, we relate to Joseph's situation. Innocent of wrongdoing, we suffer with thoughts of self-pity. If we only read verse 20, which says, "And he was there in the prison," we experience feelings of defeat and weakness. However, the next verse says: "But the Lord was with Joseph and showed him mercy. . . ."

The writer of Psalm 112:4 declared: "Unto the upright there arises light in the darkness." Even in the darkness of the king's dungeon, Joseph's strong faith prevailed. God gave Joseph favor with the jailer, and again he rose to the position of chief prisoner, second only to the jailer. When forced to be a slave, Joseph became the best slave he could be. When forced to become a prisoner, he became the best prisoner he could be. With the knowledge that God is with us, wherever we find ourselves, we too can rise to the top because we are among the "upright." Because of our faith in God, there will "arise light in the darkness."

Joseph's light arose when the Pharaoh's butler and baker were placed in the same prison for offending the king. Both men, during the same night, had dreams that troubled them. Joseph was assigned to serve them. Hearing their troubling dreams, he told them, "Do not interpretations belong to God? Tell them to me, please" (Genesis 40:8).

The butler's dream was interpreted with vindication and restoration, while the baker's dream was interpreted with a message of doom. In three days the butler would be restored to his place and the baker would be killed. Joseph's hope for freedom rested in the butler who would soon stand beside Pharaoh again. Joseph told the butler, "Remember me when it is well with you, and please show kindness to me; make mention of me to Pharaoh, and get me out of this house" (v. 14).

Some of the deepest hurts come just as we think things are getting better. Satan kicks us around by providing a little encouragement. We grasp for any sign of improvement. The slightest ray of hope becomes a fantasy of deliverance. But Satan is more than happy to provide brief periods of exhilaration in order to increase more suffering later. For Joseph, the following weeks must have been a slow slide into depression, for "the chief butler did not remember Joseph, but forgot him" (v. 23). As the last ray of hope flickered and died, Joseph must have experienced the darkest days of his life.

However, Joseph did not become overwhelmed by his circumstances. Faithfully performing the tasks assigned him, his strength of character and trust in God could not be doused. No matter how gloomy our days or how low our emotional state, our character and faith can remain constant.

Dawn Arrives

Everything about morning spells newness. To see the sun rise in the east with brilliant streaks of red and orange is spellbinding. Birds greet the rising sun with a variety of songs. Our cockatiel in its cage joins the chorus in welcoming dawn. After two full years the dawn for Joseph must have been refreshing beyond imagination. As the jailer awakened Joseph, he said something about Pharaoh, a dream, a bath, and new clothes. Rushing through the process of cleaning the grit of the dungeon from his body, Joseph must have thought, _The butler remembered, the butler remembered!_

Through the intervention of God, Joseph interpreted Pharaoh's dreams to foretell seven years of plenty followed by seven years of famine. Joseph followed this interpretation with wise counsel (also obviously from God) for a plan to take advantage of the years of plenty in preparation for the years of famine. Pharaoh decided that Joseph was obviously the man to see Egypt through such a time, when he declared:

> "Can we find such a one as this, a man in whom is the Spirit of God?" Then Pharaoh said to Joseph, "Inasmuch as God has shown you all this, there is no one as discerning and wise as you. You shall be over my house, and all my people shall be ruled according to your word; only in regard to the throne will I be greater than you" (Genesis 41:38-40).

Joseph's world changed in one day. He awoke in filthy rags in a dungeon and went to bed in royal robes in a palace. He awoke a slave in the morning and laid his head at night to rest with more authority than all of Egypt's generals combined. The Bible says, "But those who wait on the Lord shall renew their strength; they shall mount up with wings like eagles, they shall run and not be weary, they shall walk and not faint" (Isaiah 40:31). Joseph held to his character and faith until God's plan was fulfilled.

It would be several years before Joseph would fully understand why God allowed these turn of events in his life. When his brothers came to Egypt for food, everything began to make sense.

Isn't that how it usually works in our lives? After we go through hard times, we look back and say, "Aha!" We see that God really was in charge and was working for our good even when we had lost everything. Joseph would tell his brothers in Genesis 45:7, 8: "And God sent me before you to preserve a posterity for you in the earth, and to save your lives by a great deliverance. So now it was not you who sent me here, but God."

Joseph's strength of character enabled him to wait upon the Lord during times of suffering. Because of this strength, he could forgive his brothers for their role in the fulfillment of God's plan.

Strength of a Calling

It was a warm summer evening in 1972. Blowing out the kerosene lamp, I settled into my cot covered with coal dust to listen to the Cincinnati Reds game on the radio. At the time, I was working two jobs trying to make enough money to leave the hills of Kentucky and find work in Lexington. I worked for a contractor building houses during the day and slept in a dirty coal-mine shed at night while working as a night watchman. The Reds were in a hot pennant race, and I rarely missed their games. I had been saved less than two years and filled with the Holy Spirit only six months. Growing up in a preacher's home, I had no inclination toward the ministry.

Just as clearly as one would hear an audible voice, I heard the Lord speak to my spirit a single word: "Pray!" Still interested in the baseball game, I hesitated. "Pray!" the Lord commanded a second time. I turned off the radio and knelt in the coal dust. The Holy Spirit immediately fell upon me with a force I had not experienced before, and I began to pray in tongues.

After praying in the Spirit for some time, the Lord spoke to me again just as clearly as the first time. This time the command was to take my Bible and go outside the shed. Still moved upon by the Holy Spirit, I picked up the old Bible my mother had given me. For the next two hours I walked the crest of the mountain, clutching my Bible and speaking in tongues in a manner not unlike someone preaching. Later, I found myself back at the shed, trembling under the power of the Holy Spirit's anointing. I had been called to preach the gospel of Jesus Christ.

Since that spiritual experience, I have never doubted God's call. Throughout my 26 years of ministry I have reflected on that event with rejoicing and a sense of peace. There have been a few times when the memory and impact of that experience kept me going. If I had not had that definite, unquestionable call of God, my life would have taken a different turn. Now when problems and difficulties arise, I have the certainty that God called me to do His work.

This is precisely what a calling is all about. It is not a unilateral, selfish decision. It is a distinctive understanding and agreement between the Caller and the one being called. According to Romans 11:29, "The gifts and the calling of God are irrevocable." Although we may try, we cannot, and God will not, nullify His call. Our calling then becomes a source of joy in the good times and an anchor in the hard times. With each burdensome storm, God gives us strength to spread our wings and mount above it.

A Logical Calling

Carl came from a long line of Pentecostal preachers. Beginning with his great-great-grandfather, the sons in the family preached the gospel. As a child, Carl often imitated his father's preaching with skill and deftness. Everyone assumed that he would pursue this type of ministry. They encouraged and even pressured him to follow the footsteps of other family members in the ministry. He was more than happy to oblige, considering all of the attention it brought him.

Then came his teenage years—those terrible teenage years when Carl began to think for himself. One Sunday afternoon when his family gathered at their grandmother's house for dinner, he announced, "I want to be an engineer." A hush came over the room. Uncle Chuck dropped his fork with a large piece of pie still on board. Granny's false teeth chattered, and Carl's mother's face reddened. With a loud, quivering voice she said, "Carlton, you've been called to preach, and so help me, that's what you're going to do, or I'll take your daddy's belt to you!"

A godly heritage does not guarantee a calling. Only God's purposeful and intentional selection communicates a calling so personal no one can deny.

A Rise to Weakness

Circumstances placed Moses in a strategic position to become the deliverer of Israel. Because of Pharaoh's death sentence of every male child in Israel, Moses' birth was concealed for three months. When his mother could hide him no longer, she placed him in a small basket and set it adrift in the Nile River among the reeds. Through the providence of God, Pharaoh's daughter found the basket with the baby inside. Exodus 2:1-9 relates the story of how God intervened to save Moses' life by providing his own mother as nursemaid during his critical formative years.

As a member of Pharaoh's house, Moses grew up with the prestige and power associated with royalty. However, his strength was revealed in adulthood with a desire to ease the suffering of his people. When he set out to fulfill his calling, his strength and leadership were tested.

There are real problems with position and power derived from human relationships. First of all, they give a false sense of self-reliance and confidence, especially if the relationship is family-oriented. More importantly, however, is the fact that anything accomplished through this kind of authority and power robs God of His glory. This is why God has generally chosen the weak and powerless to become instruments in the performance of His will.

Our most gallant attempts at being strong appear so minuscule when we see the overall picture of God's plan. This is probably how Moses viewed his first efforts of defending his people (see Exodus 2:11-15). With one Egyptian dead, one abusive beating avenged, and an escape into the wilderness, Moses must have thought, *Some calling . . . some deliverer!* Not only had he failed to ease the suffering of his people, but he had also lost the advantage and strength of being a member of Pharaoh's household. He probably considered himself lucky to escape with his life.

At the age of 40, Moses fled to Midian, where he met his wife Zipporah and began tending sheep for her father, Jethro. He would remain here for the next 40 years—a man of little consequence.

God has a plan for every calling—a due season for His plans to take shape. Waiting patiently for God's timing tests our strength. With each test we ask ourselves three questions:

1. What is the problem?
2. What is the solution?
3. What is my part in this solution?

Normally we jump to the third question with our spiritual hammer, screwdriver, or roll of duct tape to fix the problem as we would fix things around the house. We think we know God's intentions in the situation.

Between question 1 and question 3 is where we find the strength of God's calling. Moses learned that his strength, bolstered as it was by his relation to Pharaoh, was not sufficient. He spent many years reflecting upon that failure while tending his father-in-law's sheep.

Elements of a True Calling

Whatever strengths and advantages Moses had acquired diminished. He went from a son in Pharaoh's house to a shepherd in the wilderness . . . from wearing robes of royalty to raiment that reeked of sheep. His former days of leisure in the palace were gone; now he spent long hours laboring in the fields. But God was still in control. These twists and turns brought him near Mount Horeb (see Exodus 3; 4).

This Biblical account of God's call to Moses is composed of five elements. These same elements were present in my calling and in the calling of several others who have shared their experiences with me. Together, they compose a process of identification and validation from which the strength of calling flows.

1. *Interruption.* There is something hypnotic about life's routines. We go along on the central path in spite of what takes place in the margins. In the margins of life, however, we find God presenting Himself to us, drawing us away from the routine. When God spoke to Moses from the burning bush, He drew him aside. Moses stepped away from his routine.

> The Angel of the Lord appeared to him in a flame of fire from the midst of a bush. So he looked, and behold, the bush was burning with fire, but the bush was not consumed. Then Moses said, "I will now turn aside and see this great sight, why the bush does not burn." So when the Lord saw that

he turned aside to look, God called to him from
the midst of the bush and said, "Moses, Moses!"
And he said, "Here I am" (Exodus 3:2-4).

Notice the sequence of events. God first ignited the
fire within the bush and observed Moses' response.
When Moses "turned aside," He called to him from the
burning bush. I believe this sequence is important in
understanding the dynamics of God's calling today. To
communicate an important message, God must first get
our attention. For some, God's call comes in the midst
of sickness or trial; for others, it comes during times of
private devotions or fervent worship. In every case, God
must have our undivided attention.

When God sees that we are willing to interrupt our
harried routine and focus on Him, then He calls us.

2. *Dialogue*. For Moses, dialogue came with God's calling his name twice. For me, God commanded me in my
spirit to pray. Once begun, dialogue continues for life.
We may occasionally stray too far to hear His voice, or
we may even try to ignore it. But once heeded, the voice
of God will not be silenced. God said to Moses, "I will
be with your mouth and teach you what you shall say"
(4:12). Even when Moses resisted because of being
"slow of speech and slow of tongue" (v. 10), God would
not relent. Instead, He assigned Aaron to assist Moses

and promised, "I will be with your mouth and with his mouth" (v. 15).

The excesses and tragic mistakes of those called of God come about when they either ignore God's voice or they misinterpret it. Moses fell prey to this when he struck the rock God commanded him to "speak to" (Numbers 20:7-13). For this disobedience, neither he nor Aaron was allowed to enter the Promised Land. It is important to note that although it is a dialogue—a two-way conversation between God and man—God's word must not be taken casually.

3. *Sanctifying.* The third element in the call of Moses was a sanctifying of the event. Moses did not have any real knowledge or understanding of the God of his fathers. God therefore initiated this meeting by engendering four basic sanctifying qualities: caution, reverence, recognition, and awe.

Moses was told pointedly, "Do not draw near this place." Then God said, "Take your sandals off your feet, for the place where you stand is holy ground" (Exodus 3:5). Moses was not yet aware of who was speaking to him. Then God declared, "I am the God of your father—the God of Abraham, the God of Isaac, and the God of Jacob" (v. 6). Moses suddenly became aware of the seriousness of this interruption because the verse continues by saying, "And Moses hid his face, for he was afraid to look upon God."

Just as God cautioned Moses about coming too close, we should also be cautious when we sense that God is calling us. No one should enter His presence in a flippant manner. To be reckless in our approach to God is to invite His correction. This is especially true when God is calling us into service for Him.

Many years ago, I attended a service where several men were receiving their ordination credentials in the Church of God. Two men in the group captured my attention because of the stark differences in their demeanor. One was weeping. Humbly and tearfully, he accepted the office bestowed upon him by the church. Another man laughed as he casually received the same honor. There was no sense of sobriety or caution in his actions. Today, the man who wept still preaches and the man who laughed has long ago ceased to heed God's call. Caution is not just advised when accepting God's call, it is demanded.

Reverence is an equally important quality in accepting God's call. Pride or haughtiness before God is foolish. I have observed men and women who feel that they did God a favor by accepting a call to preach the gospel. Make no mistake—God requires humility and reverence from everyone He calls.

The most powerful part of the sanctifying of the call is the awareness of the God in whose presence we stand. If caution and reverence have not brought us to our knees, recognition of the presence of God surely will. I am reminded of Isaiah's meeting with God and his response:

> I saw the Lord sitting on a throne, high and lifted up, and the train of His robe filled the temple. . . . So I said: "Woe is me, for I am undone! Because I am a man of unclean lips, and I dwell in the midst of a people of unclean lips; for my eyes have seen the King, the Lord of hosts" (Isaiah 6:1-5).

Moses' response mirrors that of Isaiah. He hid his face, unable to look upon the presence of God. Any encounter with God, especially one that summons you and me to His service, should be met with this kind of emotion.

4. *Struggle.* The fourth element in Moses' calling was a struggle between him and God. In reading the text, it seems that this struggle was adversarial—Moses struggling against God. However, in considering the awesome task to which Moses was being called, it becomes clear that this struggle was more with himself than with God. Five times Moses made excuses that indicate his reluctance in accepting God's call. With each excuse, God assured him that he was chosen for this work.

Moses used the argument of insufficiency when he asked, "Who am I?" to which God responded, "I will certainly be with you" (Exodus 3:11, 12). Then he used the argument of ignorance when he asked, "Indeed, when I come to the children of Israel and say to them, 'The God of your fathers has sent me to you,' and they say to me, 'What is His name?' what shall I say to them?" (3:13). God's response to this question was, "I AM WHO I AM" (3:14). Moses also argued: "But suppose they will not believe me or listen to my voice" (4:1). To this question God responded with manifestations of miraculous power in and through Moses that would verify to Israel and to Pharaoh that he had been sent by God (4:2-9).

Again Moses raised the issue of personal limitations when he said, "I am slow of speech and slow of tongue" (v. 10). But God said, "I will be with your mouth and teach you what you shall say" (v. 12). Finally, Moses prayed for God to send someone else (v. 13). God became angry with this request, and gave Moses the assistance of his brother, Aaron. But the call had been issued, and Moses was without further excuse.

We should not be too critical of Moses for wrestling with God. Knowing our own imperfections better than anyone else, this may be a normal response when summoned into service for a perfect and holy God. It should provoke us to do some soul-searching and questioning of our ability and worthiness. We must remember that God's call is not based upon worthiness or ability. God calls, and we should not question His will.

5. *Acceptance.* The final element in the call of Moses is one of humble acceptance of the challenge placed before him. With no further discussion, Moses left the presence of God to meet his brother, Aaron, and bid farewell to Jethro, his father-in-law. He accepted the call and traveled to Egypt as God had instructed. Not only would he become the deliverer of God's people, but he would also become the vehicle God would use to reveal His law, His worship, and His will concerning Israel.

The Source of Strength

This was the same Moses who failed in his earlier attempt to relieve the suffering of his people. If anything was different in Moses, it was probably the fact that he was not half as sure of himself as he had been in Pharaoh's house. He saw himself as a shepherd of sheep more than a deliverer of Israel. But that is what God wanted.

Today God is not interested in warriors—He is interested in weaklings. Warriors earn glory for themselves, but weaklings give all the glory to God. When God calls you

and me to a particular service for Him, we must be care-
ful not to flatter ourselves by thinking that God saw our
greatness. The opposite is true. God saw Moses and me
as men who had failed miserably in our own strength,
but He chose Moses and me because of our weaknesses,
to become His instruments of strength.

6

Strength
of Commission

For many years an old stump stood in the front yard of a family home. Almost every morning the mother of four sons who lived there asked her sons to remove the old stump because it was an eyesore. The sons agreed, but never made any attempt to remove the stump. Years passed and only one son was left at home. The first morning the mother and son were alone at the breakfast table, she again requested for the stump to be removed. To her surprise and delight, that afternoon he backed the tractor up to the stump, pulled it from the ground and into a nearby field. At the dinner table she asked her son, "Why did you finally remove the old stump after all these years?"

"I just realized today that you were really talking to me when you asked us boys to remove it." Commission is accepting the charge of a task. It is sometimes the most difficult part of becoming strong.

The Weakness of One

In looking at the strength of commission, I want to examine Gideon, one of the judges in the Old Testament (Judges 6—8). Gideon was not a brave man. He was not secure in filling the role God called him to fill. Our first glimpse of him is in a winepress threshing wheat and hiding from the Midianites. Threshing wheat requires the wheat to be tossed into the air so the wind can carry away the chaff. This is difficult to do in the confines of a winepress because there is not much wind blowing. In this winepress the Angel of the Lord appeared to Gideon and said, "The Lord is with you, you mighty man of valor!" (Judges 6:12).

Gideon's response in verse 13 conveys fear: "O my lord, if the Lord is with us, why then has all this happened to us?" Did you notice Gideon's use of the word *us*? He deflected the Angel's words from himself to all of Israel. However, the Angel had spoken directly to Gideon—challenging him to a task.

The next words of the Angel of the Lord are, "Go in

this might of yours, and you shall save Israel from the hand of the Midianites. Have I not sent you?" Quickly Gideon responded, "O my Lord, how can I save Israel? Indeed my clan is the weakest in Manasseh, and I am the least in my father's house" (vv. 14, 15). This statement reveals insufficiency—something you and I can relate to.

That same night God told Gideon to tear down the altar to Baal that his father had built, along with the wooden image beside it. He was instructed to build a proper altar to God and use the wood from the image for a burnt offering to God. In fear of "his father's household and the men of the city" (v. 27), Gideon performed this task at night. Gideon was not the valiant hero we envision.

The following morning when the men of the city found out who destroyed the altar to their god, they came to Gideon's father's house to kill him. Gideon hid inside while his father spoke to the angry mob in his defense (vv. 28-31).

Gideon's use of the fleece (vv. 33-40) is another indication of his doubts in his own ability. I remember, as a boy, being taught in Sunday school the importance of placing a fleece before the Lord. It was not until I studied the passage as a minister that I saw this as an act of doubt, rather than faith. Twice he tested God by using a fleece of wool and the morning dew. First he asked God to make the fleece wet with dew and the ground dry. The next morning he asked God to make the fleece dry and the ground wet. He was asking, "God, are You sure You have the right man for this job?" When God answered "Yes," Gideon asked again, "Are You really sure?" Again, God answered, "Yes."

This is not exactly a great beginning for a Biblical hero. Gideon is not like David who stood before Goliath; he is not like Samson who feared neither man nor beast. Gideon is a more accurate role model for us than either David or Samson, who had uncommon callings and abilities. They stand out as extraordinary in the midst of the ordinary. But Gideon was an ordinary man who was called of God to do an extraordinary thing. I can see myself more easily in Gideon's shoes than in either David's or Samson's.

The story of Gideon is not the story of strength, but the story of weakness for a purpose. Where David and Samson are seen as being strong in faith and physical strength from their youth, Gideon is weak and must learn to rely on God for strength.

Even up to the point of entering the battle, Gideon was aware of his weakness and fear. God told Gideon, "But if you are afraid to go down, go down to the camp with Purah your servant, and you shall hear what they say; and afterward your hands shall be strengthened to go down against the camp" (7:10, 11). Gideon acknowledged his fear by doing exactly what the Lord suggested. The conversation between the Midianite soldiers is recorded in verses13, 14:

> And when Gideon had come, there was a man telling a dream to his companion. He said, "I have had a dream: To my surprise, a loaf of barley bread tumbled into the camp of Midian; it came to a tent and struck it so that it fell and overturned, and the tent collapsed." Then his companion answered and said, "This is nothing else but the sword of Gideon the son of Joash, a man of Israel! Into his hand God has delivered Midian and the whole camp."

Reassured of God's will and direction, Gideon left the camp of the Midianites ready to act upon God's command. If God had used only people like David and Samson, most of us would not have an example of what God could do through us. It is men like Gideon who motivate us by demonstrating how God can use us in spite of our weaknesses. Gideon stands as a testimony to the fact that God does commission ordinary people to do His extraordinary work.

The Weakness of Many

In Judges 6:16 God told Gideon, "Surely I will be with you, and you shall defeat the Midianites as one man." I want to pay close attention to God's use of the phrase "as one man." The meaning of this phrase would not be significant until God finished His preparation of Gideon and his men for the battle with Midian.

The hordes of Midian gathered together in the land of Israel as they had for the past seven years. Again the crops, herds, and homes of Israel were in jeopardy. But as this invasion was taking place, "the Spirit of the Lord came upon Gideon; then he blew the trumpet, and the Abiezrites gathered behind him" (6:34). We are not given the exact number of Abiezrites who joined Gideon, but it was probably low, considering Gideon's assessment of his tribe in verse 15: "My clan is the weakest in Manasseh." Because of the low number, Gideon sent messengers to Manasseh, Asher, Zebulun, and Naphtali in search of troops to join him in battle.

As his army began to take shape, Gideon gained confidence and optimism about the battle. With 32,000 troops gathered around him, his security also increased. But God spoke to Gideon with these words: "The people who are with you are too many for Me to give the

Midianites into their hands, lest Israel claim glory for itself against Me, saying, 'My own hand has saved me'" (7:2). Therefore, God began a process of elimination that would reduce the size of Gideon's army to suit the term "as one man" (the term used in calling Gideon).

Gideon's first response was fear, but God told him to announce to the people, "Whoever is fearful and afraid, let him turn and depart at once from Mount Gilead" (7:3). Gideon's army of 32,000 men was immediately reduced to 10,000—a reduction of more than two-thirds. It might be said that these 22,000 men were truthful about their fear and the remaining 10,000 men were afraid to tell the truth. But 10,000 is not a bad number. Gideon could still produce a pretty good conflagration.

> But the Lord said to Gideon, "The people are still too many; bring them down to the water, and I will test them for you there. Then it will be, that of whom I say to you, 'This one shall go with you,' the same shall go with you; and of whomever I say to you, 'This one shall not go with you,' the same shall not go." So he brought the people down to the water. And the Lord said to Gideon, "Everyone who laps from the water with his tongue, as a dog laps, you shall set apart by himself; likewise everyone who gets down on his knees to drink." And

the number of those who lapped, putting their hand to their mouth, was three hundred men; but all the rest of the people got down on their knees to drink water. Then the Lord said to Gideon, "By the three hundred men who lapped I will save you, and deliver the Midianites into your hand. Let all the other people go, every man to his place" (Judges 7:4-7).

How often do we try to "outthink" God by doing what we think is right? Gideon's reasoning seemed right: "Gather together a large army and you will have the battle well under control before it starts. Call together as many of the men of Israel as you can and surely God will be with you. After all, is there not strength in numbers?" Missing in this logic is the most important element of God's will, God's strength.

Are we not guilty of the same thing? We may know what God wants to do, but we do not know how He plans to accomplish it. When the job is completed, we realize that our efforts actually delayed God's completion of His plan.

You might ask if Gideon did not have the same number of men he started with before he summoned others from the various tribes. If so, the time it took to reduce the number of fighting men was wasted time, as well as the time it took for these men to gather together from other tribes. We can only wonder at how much time God spends undoing what we interpret as His will.

Three hundred men going up against the hordes of Midian reflects the meaning of the term "as one man" God used when he called Gideon. If Gideon had gathered a million fighting men, they would have been weaker than these 300—not because these 300 were more valiant fighters, but because God had chosen to work through 300 rather than the multitude.

The Weakness of the Plan

Torches, trumpets, and pitchers are not normal weapons. But then, this is not a normal army. The strategy was pretty shaky too—300 men trying to surround many thousands of men, hoping to surprise them (see Judges 7:16-22).

This scenario reminds me of a story I heard about two men who heard about wolf pelts selling for $500 each. Excited about the prospects of making a great deal of money, they packed up their camping gear and headed for the mountains. For several days and nights they hunted wolves, but never saw the first one. Finally, they both fell asleep around a campfire. Deep in the night after the fire had burned out, one of the men awoke to see hundreds of wolves surrounding them. He grabbed his friend by the arm and shook him saying, "Wake up, we're rich!" Only blind optimism could see any victory for these hunters . . . or for Gideon.

With torches burning inside the pitchers, they sounded their trumpets and broke the pitchers to reveal the light of the torches. As they did, they shouted, "The sword of the Lord and of Gideon!" I am not a military strategist, but you would think that a little more in-depth planning might be required here. What would happen after the pitchers broke and the shouts sounded? Other than scaring the wits out of a few hundred Midianites, what would happen when they saw so few standing against them? And what about the men in the middle of the camp of Midian who probably didn't hear the noise or see the torches? This is a plan?

Strength From Weakness

Paul said in 1 Corinthians 1:27-29:

> But God has chosen the foolish things of the world to put to shame the wise, and God has chosen the weak things of the world to put to shame the things which are mighty; and the base things of the world and the things which are despised God has chosen, and the things which are not, to bring to nothing the things that are, that no flesh should glory in His presence.

God always has a plan. His choices are made for a purpose. He knew Gideon's weaknesses when He chose him, but He wanted to reveal His own strength. God works the same way in our lives today. He selects the foolish, the base, and the despised because they are weak. We are amazed to see how God bypasses the juicy red apple to get to the apple with the worm.

Gideon is an example of the fearful—those who question God's will, finding it difficult to accept by faith what seems physically impossible. Most of us probably fall into this group. Through Gideon's weaknesses and the reduction of his army, we see that God was not looking for the bravest and strongest—He was looking for the one who would bring Him the most glory.

If God called the bravest men and equipped them with the largest armies, all the glory would belong to men, not God. In this context, strength and courage would be flaws because they would detract from the glory belonging to God. In any conflict with the world or Satan, winning is not the primary goal. The goal is to glorify God. In 1 Corinthians 6:20, Paul writes, "For you were bought at a price; therefore glorify God in your body and in your spirit, which are God's."

If greater glory comes to God through my weaknesses, then I join the apostle in saying, "Therefore I take pleasure in infirmities, in reproaches, in needs, in persecutions, in distresses, for Christ's sake. For when I am weak, then I am strong" (2 Corinthians 12:10).

The story of Gideon should prompt us to stop denying our weaknesses, stop professing strength when we know we are weak. God receives glory in the admission of our weaknesses. Let those who are afraid say, "I am afraid." Let those who are tempted say, "I am tempted." In our admission of weakness, we liberate the Holy Spirit to deliver us for the glory of God.

Resting in the strength that God had commissioned him for this battle, Gideon and his men broke their pitchers and shouted, "The sword of the Lord and of Gideon!" In a divinely induced fear, the Midianites drew their swords and killed each other (Judges 7:20-22). True to His promise, God delivered Israel "as one man"—one man with a commission.

Strength of Communion

A few weeks ago my daughter, Ashley, brought a friend home for dinner. This was not unusual because she has lots of friends and frequently has them over for dinner or for a sleepover. This young lady, however, was unique among Ashley's friends—she never stopped talking. The moment I walked through the door that afternoon, I heard a constant noise emanating from somewhere in the house. I discovered the noise was this little girl's incessant chatter.

During dinner she never ceased talking, even while she ate. The droning sound of her voice continued throughout the evening. I tried to hide in the den downstairs, but her voice managed to filtrate through the walls. If I went to my bedroom, the sound would be there. The bathroom was not a sanctuary either. I thought I would die when she asked if she could spend the night. But thankfully, my daughter and wife had other plans.

It was quite clear that this young lady was not communicating because she never stopped talking long enough for anyone else to say a word. A one-sided conversation is a monologue or a form of instruction (and sometimes torture). It is not communion.

The Art of Communion

Communion is a time of mutually sharing thoughts, emotions, ideas, and encouragement. It can be a time of sharing burdens or joys, laughter or tears. You know communion is taking place when the soul and heart of two people meet. In communion, people become real. They lay aside their pretenses . . . put down their guards . . . take off their masks and share their life. In this sense, communion probably doesn't happen often, which is sad because nothing is quite as encouraging as sharing your thoughts with a trusted friend. David expressed this type of communion when he said, "We took sweet counsel together, and walked to the house of God in the throng" (Psalm 55:14).

Communion is most beneficial when it is between the Creator and His creation. We were created for communion on this level. In Genesis we read where God came in the cool of the evening to share communion with Adam and Eve. God indicated a desire to commune with His creation when He endowed mankind with emotions and intellect capable of knowing Him. Discovering the value and strength derived from communing with the Father is a blessing beyond compare.

Daniel's Distress

Hard times bring people to church . . . and the altars. We could become cynical of the religious experiences of those who come to the Lord during these times. However, I have seen God use such times to bring people to an altar of repentance in order to grow and develop into stable Christians. In this sense, hard times can be a gift of God to bring people to a close relationship with Him. That is what took place in the life of Daniel. He and three others born of noble birth within the nation of Judah were taken captive by Nebuchadnezzar, king of Babylon. These young boys, between the ages of 12 and 15, obeyed Jewish customs and laws. They were the cream of the crop among the royalty and nobility. Nebuchadnezzar's instructions were to find "young men in whom there was no blemish, but good-looking, gifted in all wisdom, possessing knowledge and quick to understand, who had ability to serve in the king's palace, and whom they might teach the language and literature of the Chaldeans" (Daniel 1:4).

Suddenly, they were taken to a strange land and subjected to three years of forced instruction in the language and customs of the Babylonians. According to Babylonian custom, their names were changed, as recorded in Daniel 1:7: "To them the chief of the eunuchs gave names: he gave Daniel the name Belteshazzar; to Hananiah, Shadrach; to Mishael, Meshach; and to Azariah, Abed-Nego." Belteshazzar, the name given to Daniel, meant "O Bel, protect thou the hostage of the king."[1]

The name given Daniel by the master eunuch of Nebuchadnezzar reveals the plight of these young men—they were hostages. The sharpest children of the most powerful leaders in Judah were held in the palace to keep their families from inciting a revolt.

Deprived of home and family, stripped of freedom, and forced into a servant's role in a distant king's palace describes the plight of Daniel and his friends. Psalm 137 gives a vivid description of their emotional state:

> By the rivers of Babylon,
> There we sat down, yea, we wept

When we remembered Zion.
We hung our harps
Upon the willows in the midst of it.
For there those who carried us away captive asked of
    us a song,
And those who plundered us requested mirth,
Saying, "Sing us one of the songs of Zion!"

How shall we sing the Lord's song
In a foreign land?
If I forget you, O Jerusalem,
Let my right hand forget its skill!
If I do not remember you,
Let my tongue cling to the roof of my mouth—
If I do not exalt Jerusalem
Above my chief joy.

Remember, O Lord, against the sons of Edom
The day of Jerusalem,
Who said, "Raze it, raze it,
To its very foundation!"

O daughter of Babylon, who are to be destroyed,
Happy the one who repays you as you have served us!
Happy the one who takes and dashes
Your little ones against the rock!

Daniel's Discovery

    I have a rich heritage of godly parents who were con-
sistent examples to my brother, sisters, and me of sincere

prayer and communion with God. When I was in my early teens, I remember walking into the kitchen where my mother, unaware of my presence, lifted her hands in rejoicing. Though she had been busy at her work, she was still deeply involved in communion with God. Such memories remind me that I can find solace in the midst of turmoil.

Daniel must have had this kind of example. In the midst of his distress, a memory surfaced of someone going to a particular place and seeking the face of God. It may have been a family member, a friend, or a priest. But this act of communion would be his salvation, his strength.

What Daniel experienced, however, was more than a time of respite or diversion from the harshness of life—he discovered a Spirit-empowered life. Strength gained from such a prayer life is dramatically presented in one of my favorite psalms (91:1-10):

> He who dwells in the secret place of the Most High
> Shall abide under the shadow of the Almighty.
> I will say of the Lord, "He is my refuge and my
> fortress;
> My God, in Him I will trust."
>
> Surely He shall deliver you from the snare of the
> fowler
> And from the perilous pestilence.

He shall cover you with His feathers,
And under His wings you shall take refuge;
His truth shall be your shield and buckler.
You shall not be afraid of the terror by night,
Nor of the arrow that flies by day,
Nor of the pestilence that walks in darkness,
Nor of the destruction that lays waste at noonday.

A thousand may fall at your side,
And ten thousand at your right hand;
But it shall not come near you.
Only with your eyes shall you look,
And see the reward of the wicked.

Because you have made the Lord, who is my refuge,
Even the Most High, your dwelling place,
No evil shall befall you . . .

To "dwell in the secret place of the Most High" is to establish a regular prayer life in a "secret" spiritual room where only you and God commune. Upon leaving that room, you "abide under the shadow of the Almighty," meaning that God's shadow covers you.

Daniel established a pattern of prayer that was as sacred to him as a visit to the Temple in Jerusalem. Three times a day Daniel opened his upstairs windows toward Jerusalem and shared a time of communion with God. This "was his custom since early days" (Daniel

6:10). Even as a hostage in Babylon, Daniel received peace, comfort, and strength from this communion.

Daniel's Devotion

In his captivity, Daniel served the kings well and became honored in their eyes. God blessed him abundantly by giving him interpretations to Nebuchadnezzar's dreams. After interpreting a writing inscribed on a wall by the fingers of a man's hand at a party given by Belshazzar (Nebuchadnezzar's son), he was promoted to one of three governors under King Darius.

Jealous of Daniel's success, the two other governors and those under them set out to destroy Daniel. But they could not find where he had been dishonest in any way, "nor was there any error or fault found in him" (Daniel 6:4). Then they came to this conclusion: "We shall not find any charge against this Daniel unless we find it against him concerning the law of his God" (v. 5). So obvious was Daniel's devotion to God that his enemies recognized it as their only means of attacking him.

In the course of time, everyone knew Daniel's whereabouts at three specific times each day. Anyone passing on the street below could hear the voice of Daniel praying in an open window. Those waiting for official business with the governor would be told that Daniel would not be available until after his prayer time. These sessions were Daniel's strength, his life force. He would not, and could not, miss a single one.

Satan knows where our strengths are and if at all possible, he will devise ways to neutralize them. This is how he worked through the mob—the governors and satraps—whose intentions were to destroy Daniel. A regular routine of prayer gave them opportunity to launch their plot. Relying on the vanity of King Darius, they approached him with their petition:

> "All the governors of the kingdom, the administrators and satraps, the counselors and advisors, have consulted together to establish a royal statute and to make a firm decree, that whoever petitions any god or man for thirty days, except you, O king, shall be cast into the den of lions. Now, O king, establish the decree and sign the writing, so that it cannot be changed, according to the law of the Medes and Persians, which does not alter." Therefore King Darius signed the written decree (6:7-9).

What is not said here is as important as what is said. By observing Daniel's times of prayer, they knew he would succumb to their trap because of his unwavering faithfulness to prayer. This observation reveals a lot about Daniel's devotion to his time with God.

What does it take to interfere with our church attendance, Bible reading, or devotional time? A retired minister commented on rainy Sundays: "Ten drops of rain will keep 20 Christians out of church." We allow petty incidents to interfere with our privileged communion with God and His church.

Everyone knew how Daniel would meet the news of this decree, and he did not disappoint them. "Now when Daniel knew that the writing was signed, he went home. And in his upper room, with his windows open toward Jerusalem, he knelt down on his knees three times that day, and prayed and gave thanks before his God" (v. 10).

Those who sought to kill him were so sure of Daniel's actions that they "assembled and found Daniel praying and making supplication before his God" (v. 11). Darius had little choice but to carry out the prescribed punishment. He reluctantly sentenced Daniel to the lions' den with this conviction: "Your God, whom you serve continually, He will deliver you" (v. 16). King Darius was fully aware of Daniel's devotion to God. He recognized that Daniel's communion with God was his strength.

Daniel's Deliverance

I remember as a boy, seeing a picture of Daniel in the lions' den, lounging around the den, even stroking one of the lions. Now I see that scene differently with the lions witnessing a marvelous evening of communion between God and Daniel while the angel of God shuts the mouths of the lions (6:22). God was faithful to Daniel—He delivered him from the lions, but more importantly, He gave him strength of communion.

King Darius was so troubled that he did not eat or sleep. Nothing could bring him comfort and rest. Daniel, on the other hand, was enjoying a feast of fellowship with God. He dined upon the Divine Presence that nourished his soul and blessed him with rest.

When King Darius returned to the lions' den the following morning, he called to Daniel saying, "Daniel, servant of the living God, has your God, whom you serve continually, been able to deliver you from the lions?" Daniel's response was, "O king, live forever!" (vv. 20, 21). Not only were the enemies of Daniel put to death, but the greatness of God was also proclaimed throughout the kingdom, as King Darius wrote:

> I make a decree that in every dominion of my kingdom men must tremble and fear before the God of Daniel. For He is the living God, and steadfast forever; His kingdom is the one which shall not be destroyed, and His dominion shall endure to the end. He delivers and rescues, and He

works signs and wonders in heaven and on earth,
who has delivered Daniel from the power of the
lions (Daniel 6:26, 27).

Daniel's Example

Daniel went from a place of royal heritage to a place
of servitude to a foreign king. Stripped of earthly
strength, he found divine strength through communion
with God. This communion opened his heart and spirit
to relate important prophecies to future generations.
Many things God revealed to Daniel we now see as his-
torical. However, others have not yet come to pass. In
both cases Daniel's revelations are subsequent to a life
filled with the joys of consistent communion with God.

Communion was Daniel's key into the fellowship he
enjoyed with God and the success he enjoyed with man.
If communion was the source of Daniel's strength, it can
be our strength as well. We can look at Daniel's example
to develop a close communion with God that will have
an impact on those around us. But the secret is finding
that "upper room"—that regular place like Daniel
had—and praying "with [our] windows open toward
Jerusalem" (6:10). Through this communion, we will be
surprised at the strength we find in Him.

Strength of Commitment

Racing was the biggest weekly event in the back hills of Kentucky in 1966. My friend Charlie was a race-car enthusiast. At 18 he entered, ready to begin an auto-racing career.

The first few races passed without event. Charlie wasn't a "Fire-Ball Roberts," but there were signs of promise in his racing ability. Then came the fateful race. The green flag waved and they were off. At the first turn, Charlie was slightly ahead of the pack. As he entered the second turn he was well ahead. We began cheering, "Go Charlie!"

As Charlie passed the stands in the straightway, his jaws were clenched, his eyes had a wide-open glare on the track ahead, and his knuckles were white from gripping the wheel so tightly. Charlie had the look of a determined racer bent on holding his lead—and hold it he did. With every lap his lead improved. He skidded through every curve, throwing dirt from his rear tires, almost sliding into the wall. He looked like a professional, and we continued yelling, "Go Charlie!"

Charlie began to "lap" the slower drivers, which means he was passing them, placing them a full lap behind him. His expression never changed—he was in this race to win!

On the final lap, the checkered flag waved vigorously, but Charlie did not slow down. He continued speeding around the track as everyone watched in horror. Finally, Charlie drove through the fence into a clump of trees just beyond the racetrack. When the car came to a stop, Charlie climbed out, shaken but unhurt.

Later we learned that the throttle on Charlie's car stuck in the wide-open position at the beginning of the race. The brakes, not a top priority in this type of vehicle, were insufficient to slow the car down. Charlie's look of determination had actually been one of terror. Skidding around the turns had not been planned, and crashing through the fence was his only means of stopping. Charlie was committed to winning the race, but not by choice. Circumstances beyond his control committed Charlie to his course. He won the race, but not exactly as he had imagined.

Sometimes our commitments are similar to Charlie's predicament. We find ourselves in situations where all we can do is cope. Our objective changes from "winning the race" to "staying on track." Ironically, this type of situation brings God the most glory in our lives. In these situations, our primary commitment becomes trusting God as He manages the events unfolding around us.

I visualize Paul as one who was continually caught in these types of circumstances. The twists and turns of his life escorted him into uncharted territory. His faith in God became the only stabilizing factor. You might think that God was abusive to Paul to allow him to become trapped in these situations. On the contrary, Paul was well suited for this type of life.

Paul's Formative Experience

The ability to stay committed may be the product of social and formal instruction. In our early years we learn values from our family, our friends, and our environment that remain with us the rest of our lives. Beyond that, our educational system provides the foundation upon which traits like commitment are established. All of these elements were in place in the apostle Paul's life.

Paul was a Roman citizen from Tarsus. In Acts 21:39 he says, "I am a Jew, from Tarsus in Cilicia, a citizen of no ordinary city" (*NIV*). Paul was a metropolitan, a man of cities. He spent his life and ministry traveling. Bolstered by his Roman citizenship and the comforts among the throngs of the city, he adapted easily to his missionary travels.

The driving force behind Paul's commitment, however, was his deep faith and religious foundation. He was a Jew—but not just any Jew. He was a Pharisee with the finest education in Pharisaic traditions. During his youth, he spent time in Jerusalem studying his religious beliefs. Acts 22:3 describes his religious training—"at the feet of Gamaliel, taught according to the strictness of our fathers' law." Paul's pride in this training and background surfaces throughout his writing:

> If anyone else thinks he may have confidence in the flesh, I more so: circumcised the eighth day, of the stock of Israel, of the tribe of Benjamin, a Hebrew of the Hebrews; concerning the law, a Pharisee; concerning zeal, persecuting the church; concerning the righteousness which is in the law, blameless (Philippians 3:4-6).

These attributes set Paul apart from his peers. "And I advanced in Judaism beyond many of my contemporaries in my own nation, being more exceedingly zealous for the traditions of my fathers" (Galatians 1:14). Paul was so dedicated to his beliefs, committed to the task he assumed God had assigned him—to persecute the new Christian church.

I am annoyed when I hear parents say that requiring their children to attend Sunday school and church regularly will somehow turn them against the church later in life. Not only is this assumption unbiblical, it is absurd. Paul's strict upbringing obviously didn't establish a bias in his thinking against Judaism. Neither did my rather strict upbringing create a dislike for the Church of God. In both cases, commitment is rooted in childhood training.

Paul's Transforming Experience

With a strong commitment to Judaism and encouraged by belief that he was right, Paul persecuted the early church. At the stoning of Stephen in Acts 7, Paul is first mentioned by his given name, Saul, when Luke says, "And the witnesses laid down their clothes at the feet of a young man named Saul" (v. 58). Luke further says of Paul (Saul) in the following chapter:

> Now Saul was consenting to [Stephen's] death. At that time a great persecution arose against the church which was at Jerusalem. . . . As for Saul, he made havoc of the church, entering every house, and dragging off men and women, committing them to prison (8:1-3).

During his obedience to deeply held commitments, Paul came face-to-face with Christ himself. On the way to Damascus to inflict punishment upon the church, Paul had a close encounter with the Divine:

> As he journeyed he came near Damascus, and suddenly a light shone around him from heaven. Then he fell to the ground, and heard a voice saying to him, "Saul, Saul, why are you persecuting Me?" And he said, "Who are You, Lord?" Then the Lord said, "I am Jesus, whom you are persecuting. It is hard for you to kick against the goads" (Acts 9:3-5).

In one brief moment, the commitments that had guided his life were brought into question. The bright light of Paul's Pharisaic tradition suddenly became clouded. The next three days were the weakest days of Saul's life. Wrestling with his physical and spiritual blindness, he discovered that his tireless efforts to get to the top had actually taken him to the bottom. The powerful Saul became weak.

In our materialistic way of thinking, it is absurd to claim that true riches come only through bankruptcy. But that is exactly what the experience of salvation dictates. Jesus said in Mark 8:34-37:

> "Whoever desires to come after Me, let him deny himself, and take up his cross, and follow Me. For whoever desires to save his life will lose it, but whoever loses his life for My sake and the gospel's will save it. For what will it profit a man if he gains the whole world, and loses his own soul? Or what will a man give in exchange for his soul?"

Paul concurs with the words of Jesus:

> But what things were gain to me, these I have counted loss for Christ. Yet indeed I also count all things loss for the excellence of the knowledge of Christ Jesus my Lord, for whom I have suffered the loss of all things, and count them as rubbish, that I may gain Christ (Philippians 3:7, 8).

It was necessary for Paul to sink to this level of weakness in order to rise to the heights he would achieve in Christ.

The story of Paul's conversion is one of my favorite passages of Scripture. To remember our sinful state with its guilt, and then experience redemption and the purity that comes with receiving Christ, moves me to tears. Paul's conversion was dynamic. He saw the blinding light, he heard the Lord's voice, and he suffered blindness for three days. What soul-searching must have taken place during those three days of darkness . . . what conflicts must have arisen in Paul's commitments.

At the right time in Paul's distress, God spoke to Ananias in a vision and told him, "[Paul] is a chosen vessel of Mine to bear My name before Gentiles, kings, and the children of Israel. For I will show him how many things he must suffer for My name's sake" (Acts 9:15, 16). God is the master of timing. At just the right time in Paul's life, Christ met him on the road to Damascus. At just the right time in his affliction, God sent Ananias to him. When Ananias laid his hands upon Paul, we are told, "Immediately there fell from his eyes something like scales, and he received his sight at once; and he arose and was baptized" (v. 18).

The latter part of verse 18 should not be overlooked. Saul, the zealous persecutor of the church, was taken to a river and dipped in the water in a significant Jewish rite of that day. John the Baptist had denied the Pharisees and Sadducees this rite of baptism (Matthew 3:7), and evidently, none had desired to receive it from the disciples of Christ. Taking this step publicly signified Paul's acceptance of Jesus as the Messiah and renounced many of the commitments that had guided his life to this point.

If Paul's baptism wasn't enough to prove his transformation, his activities soon thereafter were. His zeal did not die—it was redirected. Saul was going to be Paul, and the good news was that he was now Paul the Christian. Acts 9:20-22 reveals his continued zeal with a new focus:

> Immediately he preached the Christ in the synagogues, that He is the Son of God. Then all who heard were amazed, and said, "Is this not he who destroyed those who called on this name in Jerusalem, and has come here for that purpose, so that he might bring them bound to the chief priests?" But Saul increased all the more in strength, and confounded the Jews who dwelt in Damascus, proving that this Jesus is the Christ.

Paul made a quantum leap, and the gulf between Pharisee and Christian was bridged. There were some dynamic new things about this man, but some of his former assets—commitment and zeal—were retained.

A New Man With Old Merits

Two factors played important roles in Paul's becoming the man we hold in high regard today—his conversion and his calling. Both of these were dramatic and powerful events. Given Paul's personality, nothing short of these experiences could have produced such a metamorphosis in his life.

First of all, his conversion was phenomenal. It was visible, aural, physical, intellectual, and spiritual. Shaken by the experience, Paul asked for the identity of the Questioner and received a spiritual revelation. When the encounter ended, everything he valued in his life became worthless. What he hated most suddenly became priceless. Three soul-searching days later when Ananias prayed for him, the scales fell from his eyes and he began to confess the once-hated name of Jesus.

Everyone born again by the grace of God can lay claim to a dynamic conversion. It may not have been as dramatic as Paul's conversion, but it is equally dynamic. Some, like my father, see visions, others hear sounds, some enter into conversations with God, and still others are physically changed in some way. All, however, have totally altered values with a confession of Jesus as Savior and Lord.

Second, Paul's calling was dramatic and powerful in that the Holy Spirit specifically chose Barnabas and him by name:

> Now in the church that was at Antioch there were
> certain prophets and teachers: Barnabas, Simeon

who was called Niger, Lucius of Cyrene, Manaen
who had been brought up with Herod the tetrarch,
and Saul. As they ministered to the Lord and fasted,
the Holy Spirit said, "Now separate to Me Barnabas
and Saul for the work to which I have called them."
Then, having fasted and prayed, and laid hands on
them, they sent them away (Acts 13:1-3).

This calling became a significant driving force that
energized a missions ministry and gave Paul a resolve
and tenacity that enabled him to endure the rigors of
rejection, persecution, and rebellion. This call eventually
led to the Pauline Epistles, which compose a large portion
of our New Testament. This calling would take Paul far
and wide at the discretion and guidance of the Holy Spirit.

The call of God changes the course of every believer's
life. Those who accept God's call know the energizing
force that motivates them for study, performance, and
endurance. There were times in my own life when I
would have considered leaving the ministry had I not
been able to reflect on that warm, summer night in
Kentucky when God called me. It was not as dramatic
as Paul's experience, but it was just as certain. The certainty of God's call has kept me on course through
temptations to leave the ministry and through heart-
breaks arising from ministry-related events.

Your conversion and calling are probably just as

meaningful and dynamic as Paul's. These special encounters with God establish a divinely directed course, but it is up to us to determine how we run and how we finish this course. Paul's strength enabled him to hold firmly to his course through the influence of the Holy Spirit. He possessed and often was possessed by the strength of commitment.

Commitment does not acknowledge another way, will not accept defeat, and cannot understand how others wane. A comparative look at the commitment of Saul the Pharisee and the commitment of Paul the Christian points out that Paul's commitment did not change, but his focus did:

+ Saul the Pharisee was unquestionably sure that the law of Moses was the last word in faith; Paul the Christian would write to the church at Rome and say, "For Christ is the end of the law for righteousness to everyone who believes" (Romans 10:4).
+ Saul the Pharisee would not rest until the enemies of his sect were imprisoned; Paul the Christian would be imprisoned himself for his faith.
+ Saul the Pharisee could not imagine another faith more righteous than his own; Paul the Christian could only accept the righteousness of Christ by faith.

Many Christians make commitments that are off-target. Commitments to the church, commitments to works of service, and even commitments to God himself are all off-target if they are founded on anything other than the Word of God. Paul's commitment to the gospel of Jesus Christ never diminished. He reminded the church at Corinth:

> I, brethren, when I came to you, did not come with excellence of speech or of wisdom declaring to you the testimony of God. For I determined not to know anything among you except Jesus Christ and Him crucified. I was with you in weakness, in fear, and in much trembling. And my speech and my preaching were not with persuasive words of human wisdom, but in demonstration of the Spirit and of power, that your faith should not be in the wisdom of men but in the power of God (1 Corinthians 2:1-5).

To Paul, there were no options—he must preach the gospel.

> I am a debtor both to Greeks and to barbarians, both to wise and to unwise. So, as much as is in me, I am ready to preach the gospel to you who are in Rome also (Romans 1:14, 15).

> For if I preach the gospel, I have nothing to boast of, for necessity is laid upon me; yes, woe is me if I do not preach the gospel! (1 Corinthians 9:16).

Through the hardships and rigors of his missionary journeys, Paul's commitment never wavered. As he related to the Corinthians:

> From the Jews five times I received forty stripes minus one. Three times I was beaten with rods; once I was stoned; three times I was shipwrecked; a night and a day I have been in the deep; in journeys often, in perils of waters, in perils of robbers, in perils of my own countrymen, in perils of the Gentiles, in perils in the city, in perils in the wilderness, in perils in the sea, in perils among false brethren; in weariness and toil, in sleeplessness often, in hunger and thirst, in fastings often, in cold and nakedness—besides the other things, what comes upon me daily: my deep concern for all the churches (2 Corinthians 11:24-28).

Paul experienced the devastation of all he had held dear. Commitment can become a rescuing strength, dragging us out of our weakness and onto solid ground. Paul's greatest strength came when he could make as strong a commitment to Christianity as he had to Judaism and the destruction of the Christians. But, as it was for Paul, commitments are only as valuable as the truth upon which they are based.

Strength of Compassion

9

A few years ago I took my family to a fast-food restaurant in Paris, Texas. As we were leaving, my 4-year-old daughter asked for a chocolate milkshake. After paying for the shake, Ashley dropped it and splattered chocolate milkshake everywhere, especially on the man standing in front of her.

Stooping to help her, my eyes scanned the man's appearance starting with his rugged, black motorcycle boots. Then I noticed his dirty jeans, black leather vest with some sort of insignia on the front, worn over a dirty T-shirt. His coal-black, shoulder-length hair and shaggy beard completed the description of a character I would not want to upset. He stood about two or three inches taller than I, and weighed about 250 pounds . . . plus he had a few friends with him. I thought I was in a lot of trouble.

Suddenly, the gruff motorcyclist reached into his pocket, pulled out a few dollars, laid them on the counter, and said, "Give this little girl another milkshake." He hadn't noticed her nervous father; he was moved by the 4-year-old with tears in her eyes.

Replacing a little girl's milkshake and redeeming a fallen creation are vastly different feats, but in each is an element of compassion. Compassion is the balm that soothes sore circumstances. It is the ability to feel a sense of sadness for someone in distress and the willingness to help. That is true compassion. Unless we intervene in the circumstances that move us, we are only sympathizing. Compassion requires a response. Compassion demands action.

The View From Above

As Eve's hand reached for the forbidden fruit, God's heart ached. As Adam took the fruit from her hand and knowingly disobeyed God, a curse was set in motion that would rest upon man and woman forever. There could be no turning back now. Everything was changed—mankind must die.

Let's imagine the following conversation between God and His Son:

"But Father," the Son asks, "what about all of Our virtues and attributes given to them. Must they die also?"

"They must," the Father replies.

"Is it impossible for us to save them?"

"All things are possible," the Father responds.

"Then what will it take?" the Son asks.

"If You would save them, You must become one of them and die in their place," says the Father.

The Son looks at the splendors of His glorious existence, His royal robes, the heavenly hosts who worship Him. Turning to the Father, He says, "I will go."

It is beyond my ability to understand what prompted the heart of God to send His Son to die for you and me. Why would God see enough value in us to allow Jesus to assume human form, much less die in human fashion that we might be saved? Could it be compassion that prompted such unfathomable acts of God? With a broken heart, God cared and intervened, and compassion was born.

The View From Below

During childhood I memorized the Golden Text of the Bible. It is the first scripture most children memorize (with the possible exception of John 11:35, "Jesus wept"). At many sporting events you see a sign held by a guy wearing a rainbow wig that reads "John 3:16." The scripture, "For God so loved the world that He gave His only begotten Son, that whoever believes in Him should not perish but have everlasting life," identifies the compassion that brought Jesus to this world. To understand the fullness of that compassion requires further study. Sending Jesus to become one of us was more than showing compassion—it was God incarnate.

Throughout the Gospels we see several instances of the compassion of Jesus.

1. *Physical affliction.*

> Now a leper came to Him, imploring Him, kneeling down to Him and saying to Him, "If You are willing, You can make me clean." Then Jesus, moved with compassion, stretched out His hand and touched him, and said to him, "I am willing; be cleansed" (Mark 1:40, 41).

Occasionally we are faced with situations that prompt us to feel sympathetic toward someone who is suffering. We whisper a prayer or offer our condolences, but that is the extent of our compassion. We care for their peripheral needs, but we can do little about the need at the center of the suffering.

This brief story in the Gospel of Mark vividly illustrates the compassion Jesus had for the leper who was afflicted with an infectious illness . . . unlawful to touch . . . hideous to look upon. Jesus, however, saw a man who was hurting from a disease over which he had no control; a man who had to leave his family and friends and stand far afield and cry, "Unclean! Unclean!" To Jesus, neither the law nor the infectious nature of the disease was intimidating. The ugliness of the afflictions of the flesh could not conceal the beauty of God in the leper. Compassion demanded that Jesus do the unthinkable—stretch out His hand and touch the oozing sores with five compassionate words: "I am willing; be cleansed."

Jesus was not overwhelmed by the needs of mankind. "And when Jesus went out He saw a great multitude; and He was moved with compassion for them, and healed their sick" (Matthew 14:14). He was never confronted with a need His compassion could not cover.

2. *Poverty and want.* Because of the nature of His incarnation, Jesus did not come to this world bathed in riches. He came to live among poor men and bring the gospel to a needy world. His sense of compassion for the poor was never dulled.

When John the Baptist asked for some assurance that Jesus was the Messiah, one of the assurances that Jesus sent him was, "The poor have the gospel preached to them" (Matthew 11:5). When the young man came to Jesus desiring to know how he might receive eternal life, Jesus instructed him to "sell what you have and give to the poor, and you will have treasure in heaven; and come, follow Me" (9:21). Jesus was aware that the poor bore greater burdens in God's service than the rich.

> Then one poor widow came and threw in two mites, which make a quadrans. So He called His disciples to Himself and said to them, "Assuredly, I say to you that this poor widow has put in more than all those who have given to the treasury" (Mark 12:42, 43).

In Matthew 15:32 Jesus revealed His compassion for a hungry multitude: "Now Jesus called His disciples to Himself and said, 'I have compassion on the multitude, because they have now continued with Me three days and have nothing to eat. And I do not want to send them away hungry, lest they faint on the way.' " What follows is not just an example of His miraculous power, but His desire to provide for their needs as well:

> And He took the seven loaves and the fish and gave thanks, broke them and gave them to His disciples; and the disciples gave to the multitude. So

they all ate and were filled, and they took up seven large baskets full of the fragments that were left. Now those who ate were four thousand men, besides women and children (vv. 36-38).

3. *Broken hearts.* "When the Lord saw her, He had compassion on her and said to her, 'Do not weep'" (Luke 7:13). Jesus wept over Jerusalem; He wept over Lazarus, and probably over other circumstances not recorded. So when He saw this widowed mother weeping over her dead son, He was moved to do something about it. The widow's son was not only a loved child, but he was also her only source of livelihood. After Jesus brought her son back to life, His compassion was extended to her broken heart as well as her uncertain future.

4. *Lost souls.* The reason Jesus came to this world was to redeem lost humanity. Everything else was secondary to His driving compassion for lost souls. "When He saw the multitudes, He was moved with compassion for them, because they were weary and scattered, like sheep having no shepherd" (Matthew 9:36). For Jesus, compassion was not an occasional emotion—He was the pure and perfect Creator walking among a corrupt creation for the expressed purpose of redeeming them back to Himself. The miracles He performed were footnotes

to His prime objective—He came to die. This compassion . . . this passion . . . was the message He came to deliver.

The View From the Cross

The Cross is the pinnacle of history. Every age before looked ahead to the Cross; every age since, looks back to the Cross. An interesting mental picture develops when you view history as a single mountain. At the crest of that mountain stands a cross with our Lord Jesus nailed to it. Looking ahead in time as well as back in history, Christ has a vantage point no one else could occupy. Jesus utters three statements of compassion from the cross that illustrate His compassion.

1. *Love.* "He said to His mother, 'Woman, behold your son!' Then He said to the disciple, 'Behold your mother!'" (John 19:26, 27). This request from the cross was simple enough. He wanted John to take care of His earthly mother after He was gone. The eternal implications, however, express a much greater scope of compassion. Jesus had instructed His disciples to "love one another; as I have loved you, that you also love one another" (John 13:34). In the very next verse He said, "By this all will know that you are My disciples, if you have love for

one another" (v. 35). This expression issuing from the cross is indicative of a greater compassion and concern held by the Lord. Christ's statements to John and Mary are relevant to Brother John Smith and Sister Mary Jones today.

In reading this expression of concern for His mother's well-being, I am reminded of another passage concerning His relationship with her:

> Then one said to Him, "Look, Your mother and Your brothers are standing outside, seeking to speak with You." But He answered and said to the one who told Him, "Who is My mother and who are My brothers?" And He stretched out His hand toward His disciples and said, "Here are My mother and My brothers! For whoever does the will of My Father in heaven is My brother and sister and mother" (Matthew 12:47-50).

As Peter has stated, "Finally, all of you be of one mind, having compassion for one another; love as brothers, be tenderhearted, be courteous" (1 Peter 3:8).

2. *Mercy*. "Then Jesus said, 'Father, forgive them, for they do not know what they do'" (Luke 23:34). In torturous pain, shame, and humiliation, Jesus expressed merciful compassion for those inflicting His pain. Given

what we know about God from His Word, we expect nothing less. God is a God of mercy. In each of the 26 verses of Psalm 136, the psalmist lauds the fact that "His [God's] mercy endures forever." The psalmist declares that God's mercy was there when the heavens were formed and when the earth was created. He claims God's mercy upon Israel and upon those of a "lowly state." Both the Old and New Testaments communicate God's mercy of God, especially the words from the cross.

From the vista of the cross, Jesus cried—"Father, forgive them" as the sins of mankind were laid upon the One who knew no sin.

3. *Acceptance.* Jesus said to the thief on the cross, "Assuredly, I say to you, today you will be with Me in Paradise" (Luke 23:43). God did not become alien to man—man alienated himself from God. Since that time, it has been God's desire to bring man back into that place of acceptance and fellowship Adam and Eve enjoyed with Him before the Fall.

The first recipient of this acceptance was one who was dying for wrongs he had committed. Jesus had said, "Those who are well have no need of a physician, but those who are sick" (Matthew 9:12). In his dying hour this sin-sick man in need of the Physician believed on

Jesus and prayed, "Lord, remember me when You come into Your kingdom" (Luke 23:42). With that simple prayer, God extended compassion and acceptance to one who deserved death. He welcomed him into His kingdom.

The View From the Throne

With the work of atonement completed and resurrection accomplished, Jesus ascended to heaven and took His rightful place beside the Father. From the throne, the compassion of Jesus flows stronger than ever before. The writer of Hebrews declared, "We do not have a High Priest who cannot sympathize with our weaknesses" (4:15). He also stated in 7:25, "Therefore He is also able to save to the uttermost those who come to God through Him, since He always lives to make intercession for them."

The compassion of Jesus conquered sin, illness, and death. Every obstacle can be conquered by the strength of His compassion. At the Father's right hand, He pleads our case passionately. Will the Father hear His pleas?

> He who did not spare His own Son, but delivered Him up for us all, how shall He not with Him also freely give us all things? Who shall bring a charge against God's elect? It is God who justifies. Who

is he who condemns? It is Christ who died, and furthermore is also risen, who is even at the right hand of God, who also makes intercession for us. Who shall separate us from the love of Christ? Shall tribulation, or distress, or persecution, or famine, or nakedness, or peril, or sword? As it is written: "For Your sake we are killed all day long; we are accounted as sheep for the slaughter." Yet in all these things we are more than conquerors through Him who loved us. For I am persuaded that neither death nor life, nor angels nor principalities nor powers, nor things present nor things to come, nor height nor depth, nor any other created thing, shall be able to separate us from the love of God which is in Christ Jesus our Lord (Romans 8:32-39).

The compassion of Jesus prompted Him to accept the weakened state of fleshly incarnation and submit Himself to death in order to redeem mankind. The strength of His compassion became our salvation and continues as strong today as ever before. Looking at our benefit from His compassion, we could proclaim with Jeremiah, "Through the Lord's mercies we are not consumed, because His compassions fail not. They are new every morning; great is Your faithfulness" (Lamentations 3:22, 23).

What compassion moves you?

Weakness
on Purpose

Several years ago a man I will call Jim became entangled in an extramarital affair. Jim and his family were respected members of the church where I served as pastor.

The news of his affair came as a tremendous shock. I refused to believe the report even though it came through another minister. I met with Jim in my office and presented the accusation to him. With remorse Jim admitted his guilt and accepted responsibility for his deeds. From the beginning he wanted to salvage his relationships with his wife, his family, and his church. He was willing to take these three steps which I consider heroic: He confessed, first to his wife, then to his family, and finally to his church.

I worked closely with Jim and his family to see them through this difficulty. During this time I learned that Jim had felt the call of God upon his life for years, but for a variety of reasons, did not feel he could accept it. At this point in his life, however, he was willing to do anything God wanted him to do. He was a broken man . . . ready to be remade by the power of the Holy Spirit. I could only remind Jim of the apostle Paul's admonition in Romans 11:29, "For the gifts and the calling of God are irrevocable."

Several years have passed, and Jim and his family not only survived that horrible time but have also grown stronger through it. Jim pastors a church, preaching the gospel he was called to do many years ago. I am sure there are scars, but it is far better to bear the scars of a battle won, than a battle lost.

Only when faced with the hideousness of our weaknesses can we accept God's exhortation in Isaiah 27:5: "Let him take hold of My strength, that he may make peace with Me; and he shall make peace with Me."

With every weakness comes a choice: we can lament our condition, pining for the days left behind; or we can look for what God is doing in the situation. God is never inactive—He is always working on our behalf. Even in a situation such as Jim and his family faced, God is at work. Paul said, "We know that all things work together for good to those who love God, to those who are the called according to His purpose" (Romans 8:28).

If Abraham had not obeyed, he would have lamented the passing of his youth and the barren womb of Sarah. Instead, Abraham believed God and in that strength, he became the father of many nations.

If Joseph had become discouraged with his brothers' treatment and his other setbacks, he could have sulked in the corner of his prison and vanished from history. Instead, Joseph held to his character, and in that strength became a ruler in Egypt and the savior of his family.

Moses had many excuses when God called him to deliver His people. If he had not accepted the call—in spite of his weaknesses—the children of Israel would have remained in Egypt's bondage.

Gideon could have fearfully cowered to God's commission to reduce his army and fight a mighty battle. Instead, he rose to the call and found God's strength to complete the work.

If Daniel had chosen to forsake the ways of his fathers and join the customs of his new home, he could have saved himself a stay in the lions' den. Instead, Daniel held to the God of his fathers and continued to abide by the laws of his heritage. In doing so, he discovered a tremendous strength—his God would not forsake him even in a strange land.

If Paul had denied his Damascus-road experience, he might have stayed with his commitments to the Pharisees and found solace in their approval. Instead, Paul chose to make a strong commitment to his Lord and Savior, Jesus Christ. The strength of that commitment encourages Christians today.

If Jesus had rejected the compassion of the Cross, we would not know the salvation we cherish today. Instead Jesus loved us enough to become flesh, to suffer and die for our sins, to take our weaknesses so that we might find strength.

Objectives of Weakness

In chapter 1, I mentioned that weakness takes two primary forms—spiritual and physical. Both forms, however, are matters of faith. But God is at work in every situation. Our obligation is to seek Him, understand what He is teaching us about life through this trial, and then simply trust Him to take care of it. Even if we don't understand, we must trust Him anyway because it is our character He is building, testing, and revealing.

1. *Character building.* Anyone who thinks the Christian experience is free from difficulty or trouble is not familiar with the New Testament. In particular, one experience of Paul's provides a strong argument for the Christian to be ready for certain peril:

> And lest I should be exalted above measure by the abundance of the revelations, a thorn in the flesh was given to me, a messenger of Satan to buffet me, lest I be exalted above measure. Concerning this thing I pleaded with the Lord three times that it might depart from me. And He said to me, "My grace is sufficient for you, for My strength is made perfect in weakness." Therefore most gladly I will rather boast in my infirmities, that the power of Christ may rest upon me. Therefore I take pleasure in infirmities, in reproaches, in needs, in persecutions, in distresses, for Christ's sake. For when I am weak, then I am strong (2 Corinthians 12:7-10).

We are not sure what this "thorn in the flesh" was in Paul's life, but we can be certain of two things: First, it was troublesome enough to be called "a messenger of Satan." Second, it took place during a time when great spiritual revelations were given to Paul.

Three times Paul asked God to remove this troublesome problem from his life, and twice the heavens were silent. The third request from Paul was met with "My silent. The third request from Paul was met with "My grace is sufficient for you, for My strength is made perfect in weakness." God was saying to Paul that it was His will for Paul to endure this "thorn in the flesh" for an unspecified period of time—perhaps forever. Paul was not distressed with this answer, however. He was more than willing to endure a weakness if the right reward came with it. "Therefore most gladly I will rather boast in my infirmities, that the power of Christ may rest upon me" (v. 9).

Perhaps during a time of weakness, God is in the process of building character within you. If you are busy lamenting your situation and complaining about God's slowness in answering as you expected, you will miss the benefit He intended for you. Notice how Paul took Satan's blow and transformed it into something more annoying to Satan than himself. "Therefore I take pleasure in infirmities, in reproaches, in needs, in persecutions, in distresses, for Christ's sake. For when I am weak, then I am strong" (v. 10). In a time of suffering, Paul's character grew even stronger.

2. *Character testing.* Many years ago I took a vocational school course in highway engineering. Part of the process of building a new highway is to test the concrete proposed for its bridges. Concrete cylinders were submitted

by the contractors and subjected to pressure tests. The data sought from these tests was the pressure point (measured in tons per square inch) at which the concrete would shatter. Every cylinder was tested until it finally crumbled.

I am so glad God does not test us in this manner. The psalmist said, "As a father pities his children, so the Lord pities those who fear Him. For He knows our frame; He remembers that we are dust" (Psalm 103:13, 14). In 1 Corinthians 10:13, we read:

> No temptation has overtaken you except such as is common to man; but God is faithful, who will not allow you to be tempted beyond what you are able, but with the temptation will also make the way of escape, that you may be able to bear it.

When we compare these passages, we see that God's knowledge is thorough and complete. He knows us, even to the very dust particles we are formed from. As a loving Father, He will allow nothing to overtake us that we are incapable of handling. He will always limit our trials and temptations based upon His omniscient knowledge of our weaknesses.

During my elementary and high school years, I thought tests were designed to find out what you didn't know about a subject. In later years and during college, I viewed tests as tools to measure my work in the class. Now I understand that if my instructors didn't care how well I knew the subject, I would not have cared either. Tests are important in measuring progress in any subject.

Tests are valuable in measuring Christian maturity as well. It pleases me when God finds me worthy of a difficult test because I know I am growing stronger in Him. James encouraged us to view our trials in this way:

> My brethren, count it all joy when you fall into various trials, knowing that the testing of your faith produces patience. But let patience have its perfect work, that you may be perfect and complete, lacking nothing (James 1:2-4).

The objective of God's occasional character testing is to allow us to observe our growth in Him, to see how far we have come, and how far we have to go.

3. *Character revealing.* The grace of God is multifaceted, functioning in accordance with particular needs of individuals. The ultimate goal of God's grace is our salvation. To achieve that goal, His grace must be revealing and convicting. This happens not out of God's vengeance, but out of His kindness.

Consider how God approached David during a dark

time in his life. In 2 Samuel 11, an accidental observation of Bathsheba bathing led David to lust, adultery, and eventually murder. When Bathsheba became pregnant with David's child, he attempted to cover his guilt by bringing Uriah, the Hittite and husband of Bathsheba, home from the battlefield so the child would be considered legitimate. When this failed, he had Uriah placed on the battlefield to be killed. God's grace came to David through the prophet Nathan:

> "There were two men in one city, one rich and the other poor. The rich man had exceedingly many flocks and herds. But the poor man had nothing, except one little ewe lamb, which he had bought and nourished; and it grew up together with him and with his children. It ate of his own food and drank from his own cup and lay in his bosom; and it was like a daughter to him. And a traveler came to the rich man, who refused to take from his own flock and from his own herd to prepare one for the wayfaring man who had come to him; but he took the poor man's lamb and prepared it for the man who had come to him."
>
> So David's anger was greatly aroused against the man, and he said to Nathan, "As the Lord lives, the man who has done this shall surely die! And he shall restore fourfold for the lamb, because he did this thing and because he had no pity."
>
> Then Nathan said to David, "You are the man!" (2 Samuel 12:1-7).

These powerful words—"You are the man"—were both condemning and caring. God was extending grace to David by revealing the error of his ways. Had God not confronted David in this manner, he would have gone through life thinking his sin had been hidden, only to face it once again in the Judgment. God was actually giving David an opportunity to judge himself before God judged him. David's response, "I have sinned against the Lord" (v. 13), brought him back into his privileged relationship with God. But David still suffered the consequences of his sin.

Revealing weaknesses that affect our character is a humbling aspect of God's grace. In His kindness, God chastens us by allowing us to see weaknesses that could separate us from Him. The Bible says, "My son, do not despise the chastening of the Lord, nor detest His correction; for whom the Lord loves He corrects, just as a father the son in whom he delights" (Proverbs 3:11, 12).

The Joys of Weakness

Possibly you have seen the statue of Atlas with his bulging muscles, awkwardly resting the world upon his shoulders. This statue is an excellent illustration of how we try to manage life within our own strength—our shoulders are strained, our backs bent, our muscles tensed, and our faces twisted from the stress of a gigantic struggle. "That's life," some would say. But it doesn't have to be that way. Jesus invites us:

> "Come to Me, all you who labor and are heavy laden, and I will give you rest. Take My yoke upon you and learn from Me, for I am gentle and lowly in heart, and you will find rest for your souls. For My yoke is easy and My burden is light" (Matthew 11:28-30).

Jesus is saying, "Those of you who think you have to carry the world upon your shoulders should come to Me. I will take the cares of this world off your shoulders and give you heavenly burdens to bear—and I will help you bear them."

There are two disadvantages for attempting to be strong in our own strength. First, the message is sent, "I don't need your help. I can handle this job all by myself." And with this attitude, no one will offer assistance. The same is true when we tell God we are self-sufficient. Second, if strength were an island, it would be a very lonely place. To present an aura of strength in spite of weakness is like saying to those around us and even to God, "I don't need you." We will then be on our own.

In admitting our weaknesses, however, God and friends

come to our aid. Labor unions are founded upon the reality of the weakness of one, but the strength of many. The church is founded upon the concept of the "body of Christ." More people relate to the feelings of weakness than to the notion of strength. Most importantly, to confess our weakness to God is to employ the strength of God. Notice again Paul's attitude in 2 Corinthians 12:9, 10, when he said he would "boast" and "take pleasure" in the weaknesses that troubled him. The reason for this boasting is simple: When we admit our weakness, God shares His strength.

An old axiom says, "Laugh and the world laughs with you; cry and you cry alone." That might be true to a certain degree in the world's way of thinking, but the Bible says:

> The righteous cry out, and the Lord hears, and delivers them out of all their troubles. The Lord is near to those who have a broken heart, and saves such as have a contrite spirit. Many are the afflictions of the righteous, but the Lord delivers him out of them all (Psalm 34:17-19).

Strong Enough for Anything

The strength we receive from God is more precious than any strength we could derive from this world. Only God's strength is lasting.

The apostle Paul expressed his philosophy of strength

in Philippians 4:12, 13: "I know what it is to be in need, and I know what it is to have plenty. I have learned the secret of being content in any and every situation, whether well fed or hungry, whether living in plenty or in want. I can do everything through him who gives me strength" (*NIV*).

Paul never boasted in his own strength—it was always the strength of God that came to him in his weakest moments. The same is true for every Christian who sets out to follow God. You and I can be strong enough for anything, and "ready for anything," as Paul said. But that strength will come at our weakest point, when we learn to say with Paul, "When I am weak, then I am strong" (2 Corinthians 12:10).

Notes

Chapter 1

[1]Edgar A. Guest, "What Counts," *Collected Verse of Edgar A. Guest* (Chicago: Riley and Lee Co., 1934) 596.

Chapter 7

[1]James Orr, ed., *The International Standard Bible Encyclopedia,* vol. 1 (Grand Rapids: Wm. B. Eerdmans Publishing Co., 1939) 782.